AF412468

Jan de Vries

Co-Relief

Afterword by
Timothy Stappaerts

Essay by
Pier Luigi Tazzi

Timothy Stappaerts,
uitgever

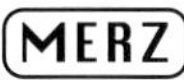

The following have contributed
to this collection of pictures:

Marina Bontridder
Peugeot 404
Agatha Bloedvloed
Augusta Futura
Futura Visavis
Ann Aalgoed
Ira Israa
Camelia Dedoodt-Prisurplas

*They are also working on equipment to shoot
themselves in the back with*

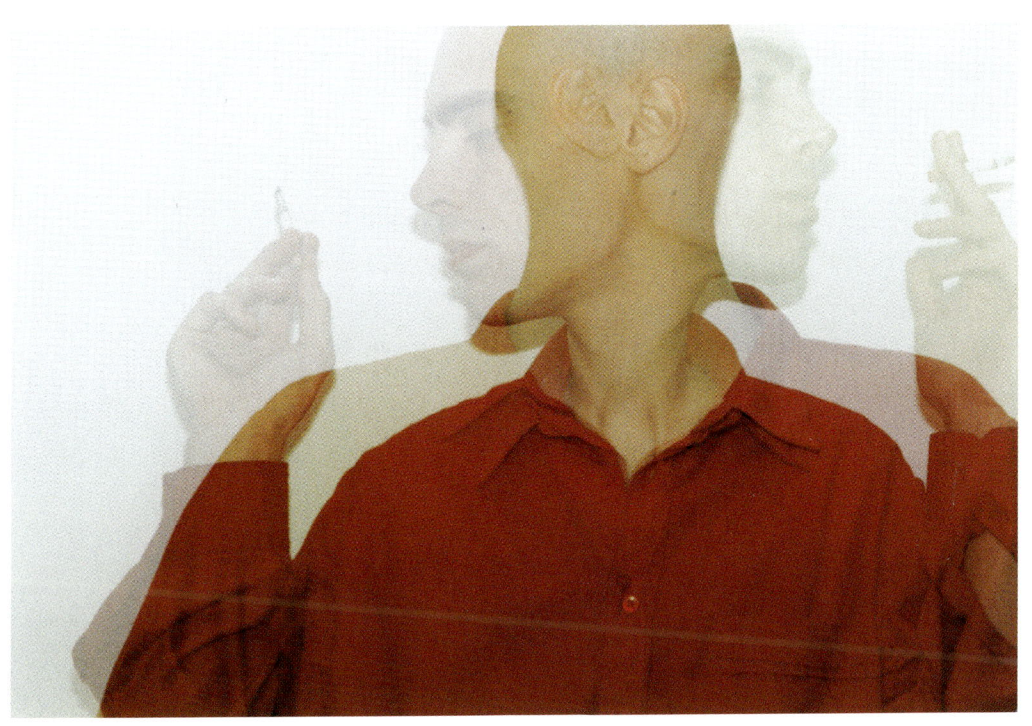

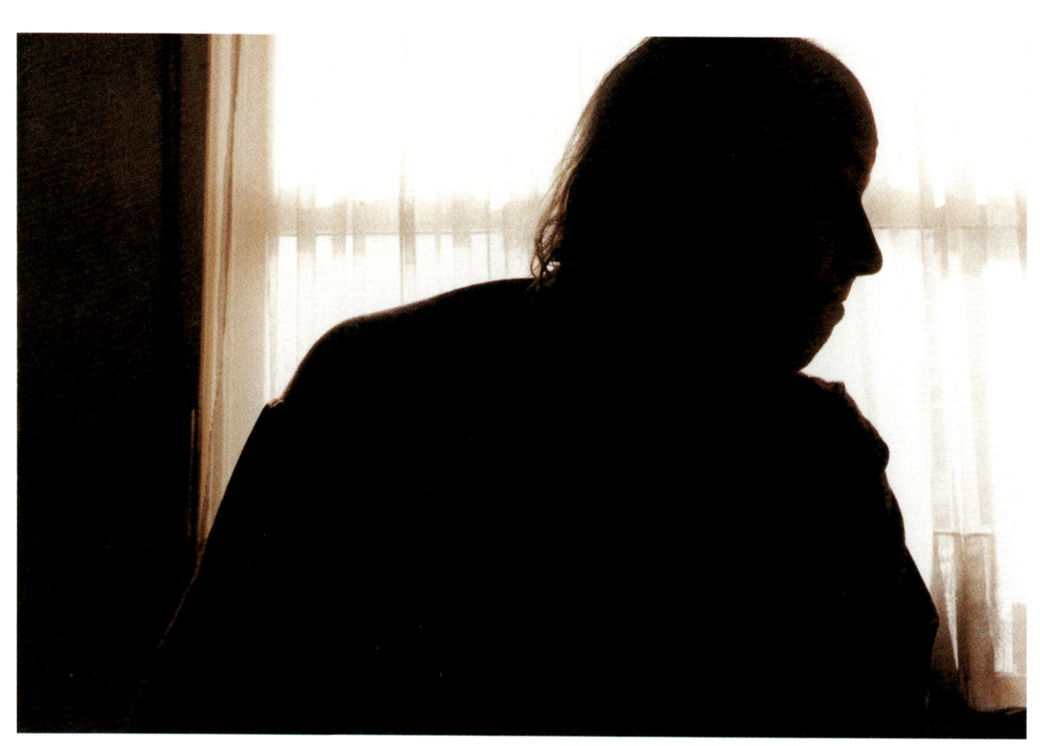

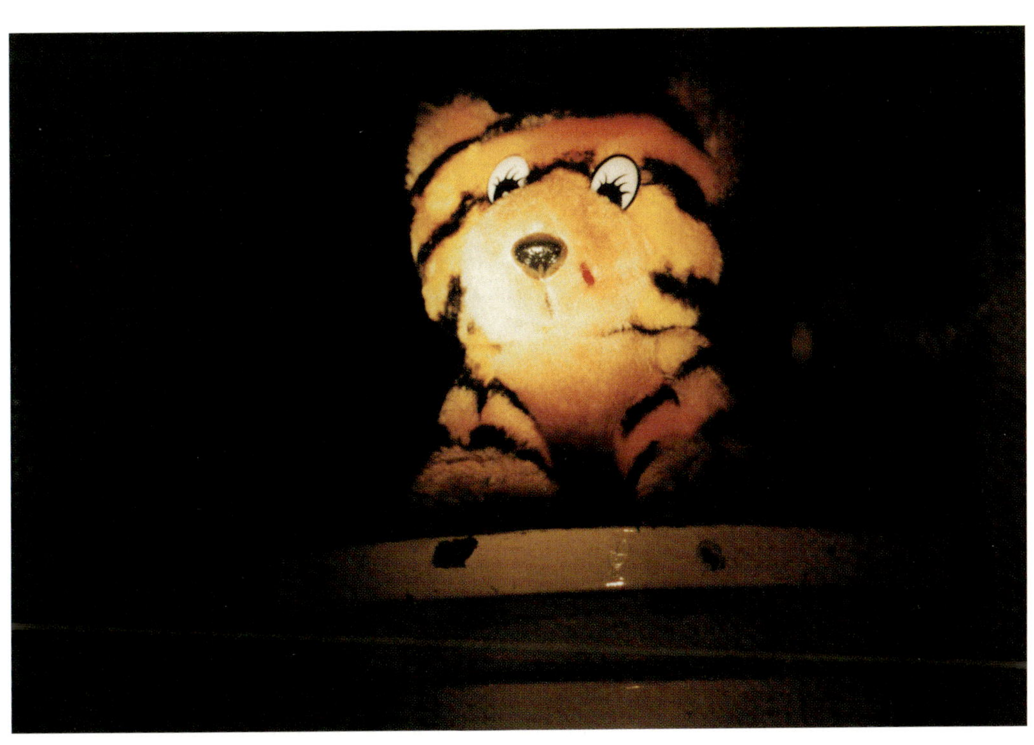

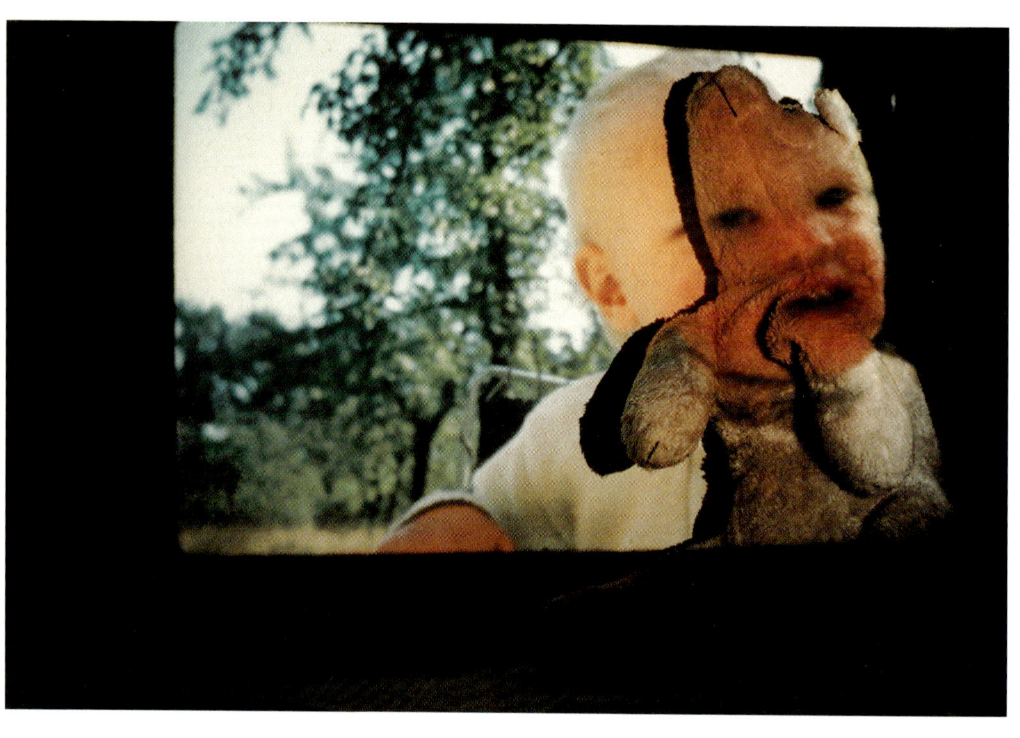

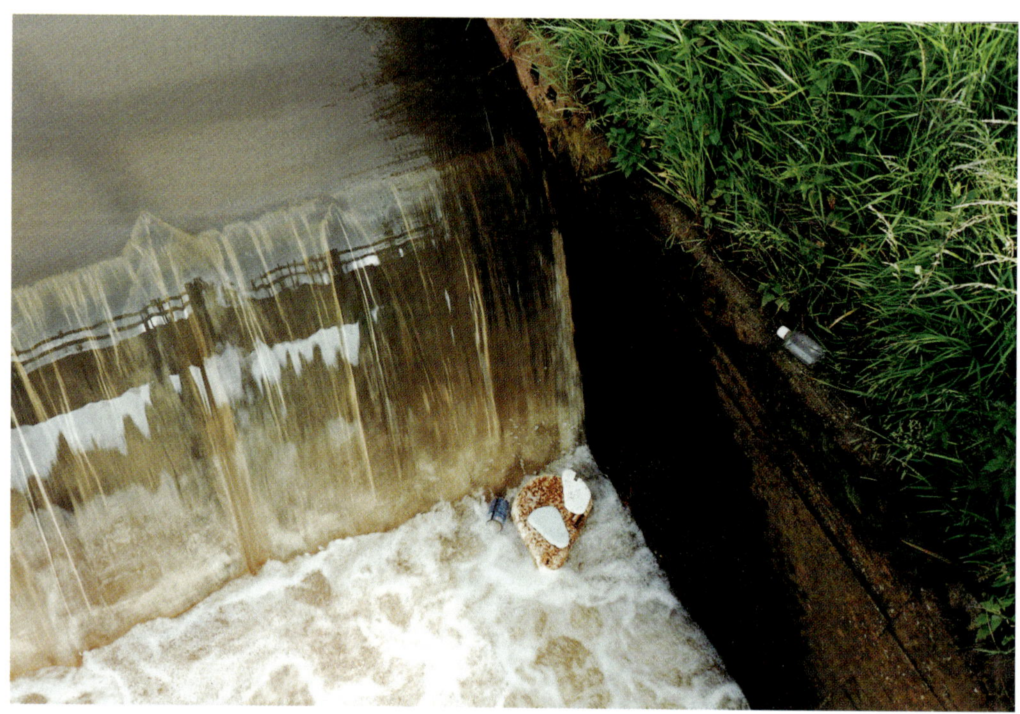

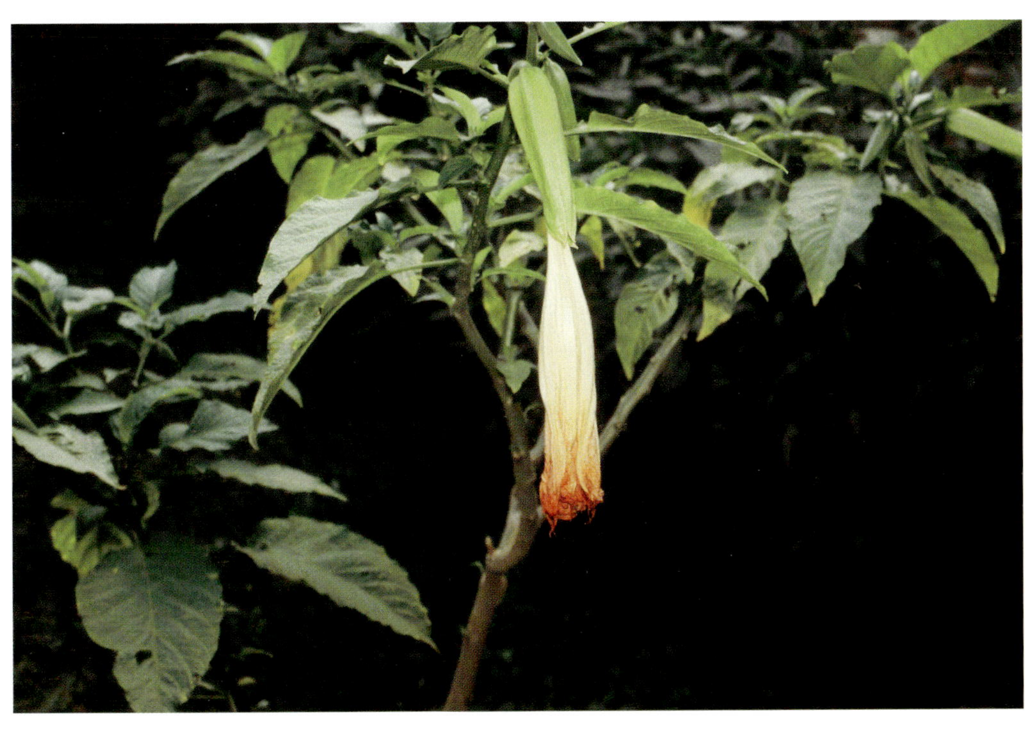

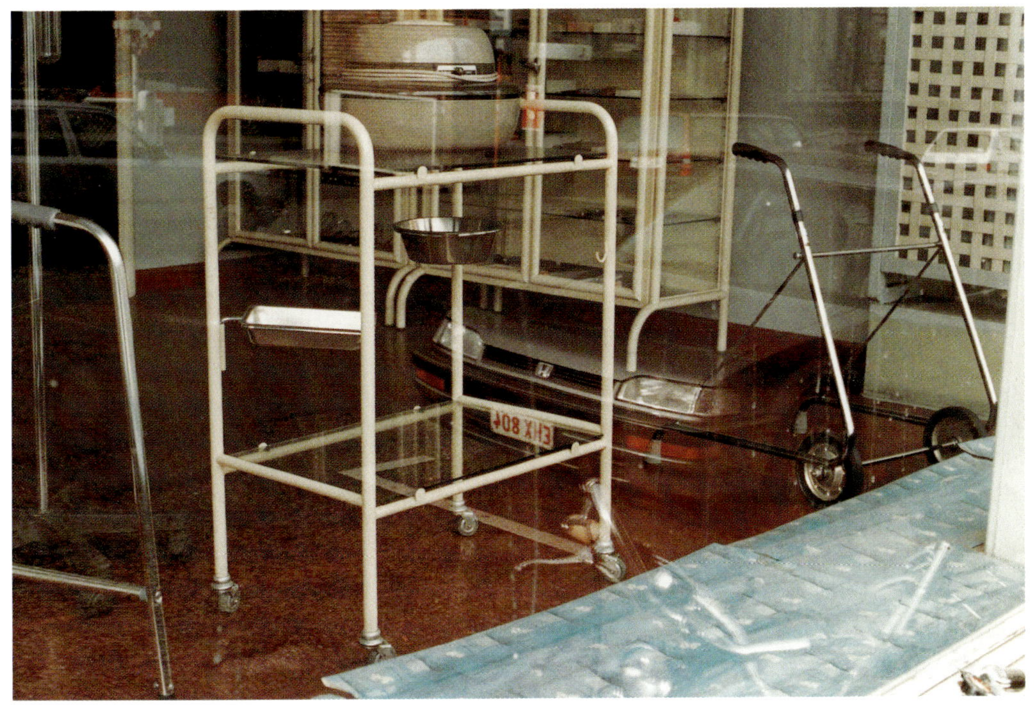

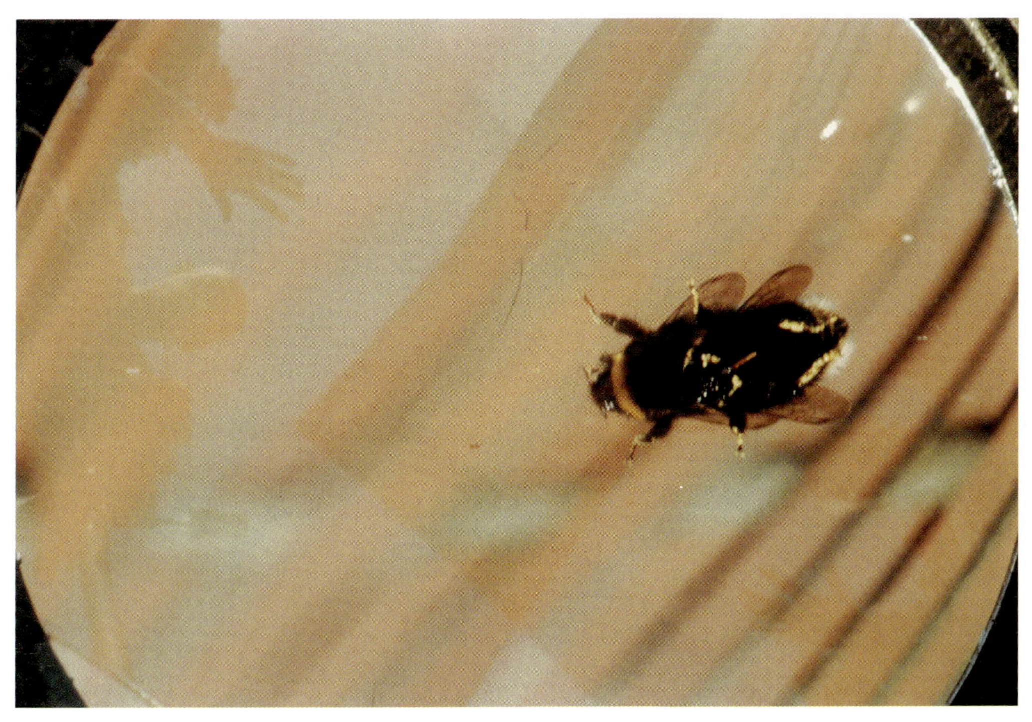

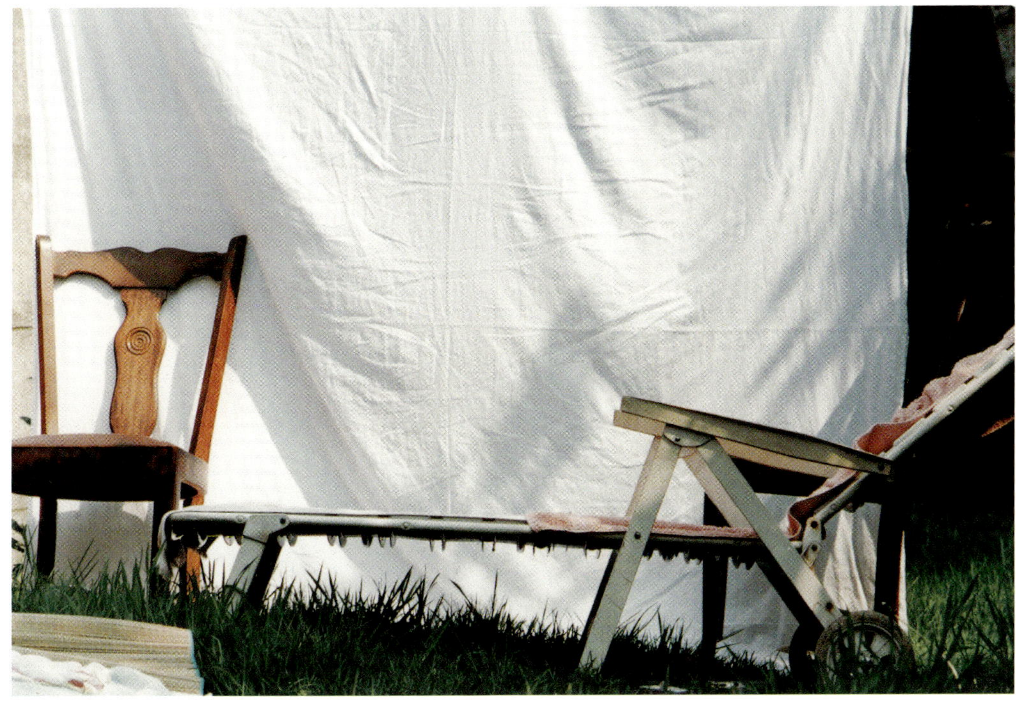

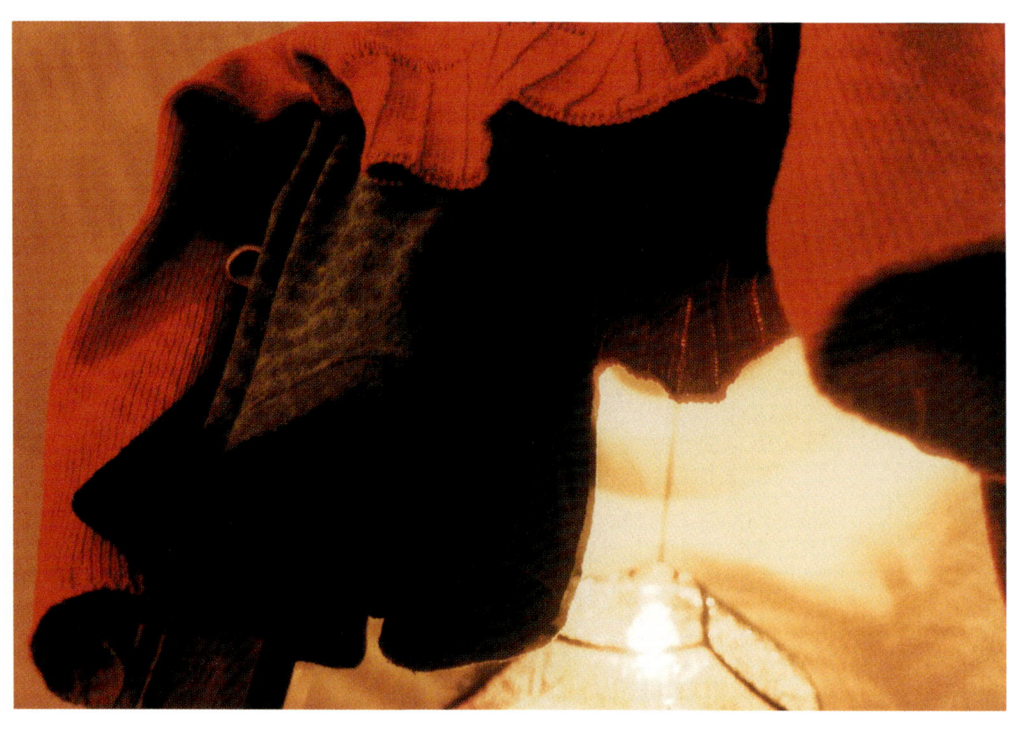

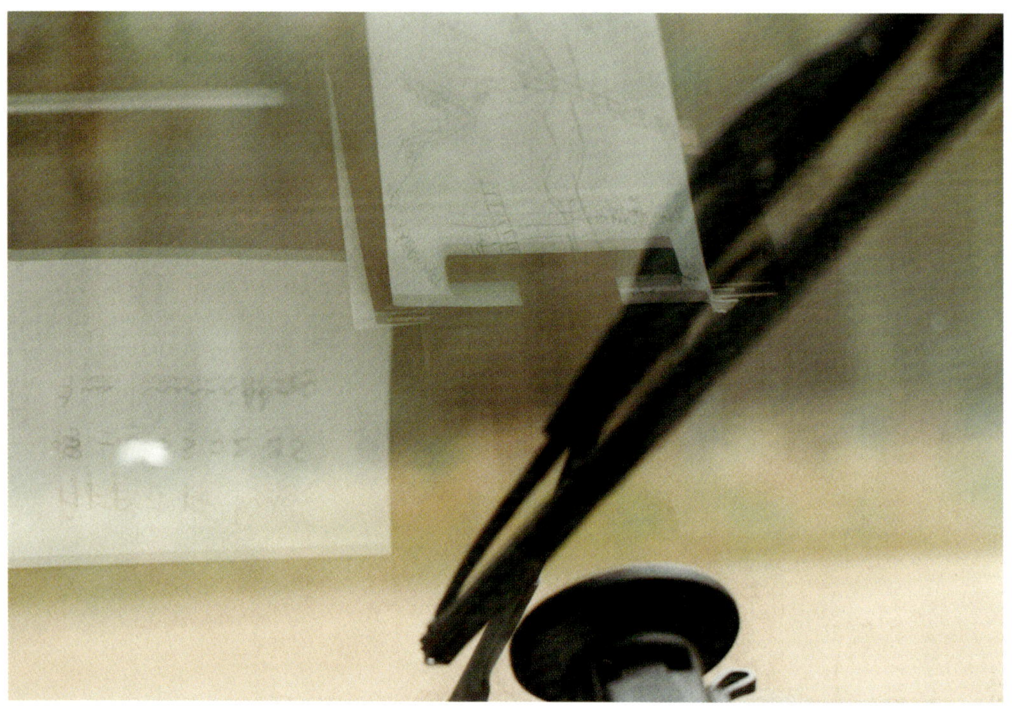

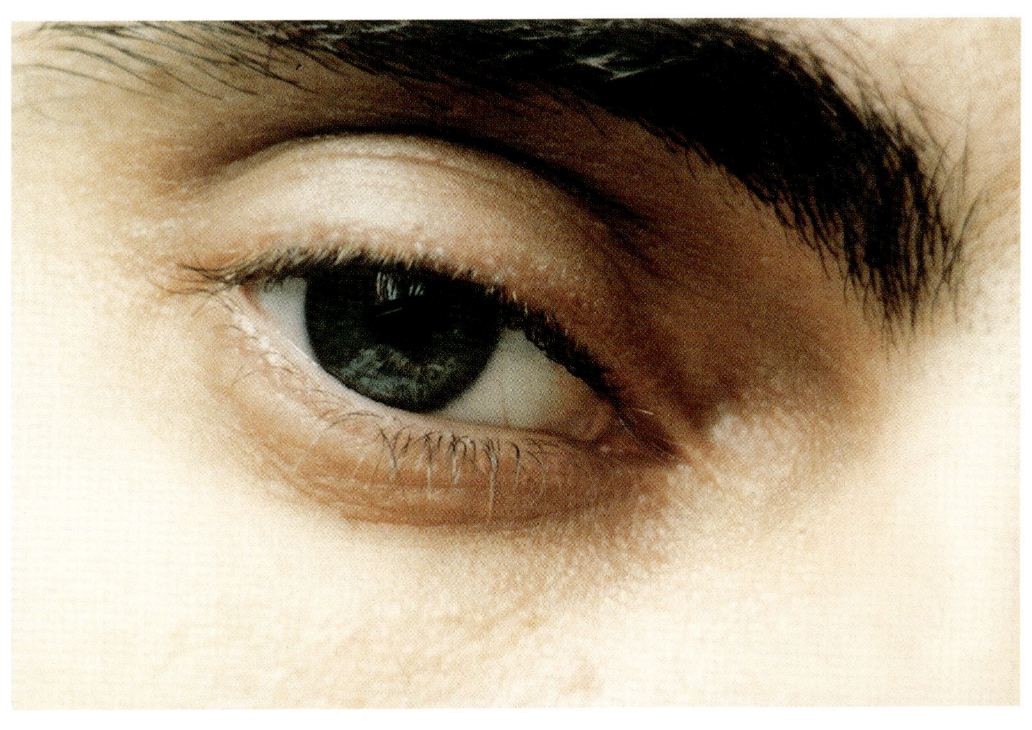

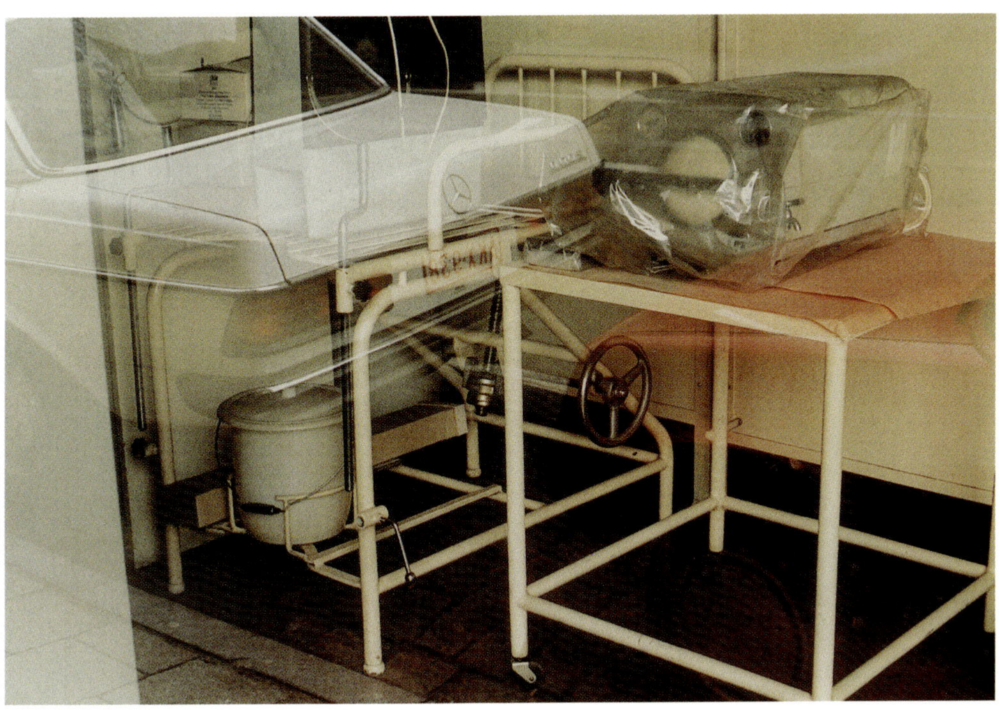

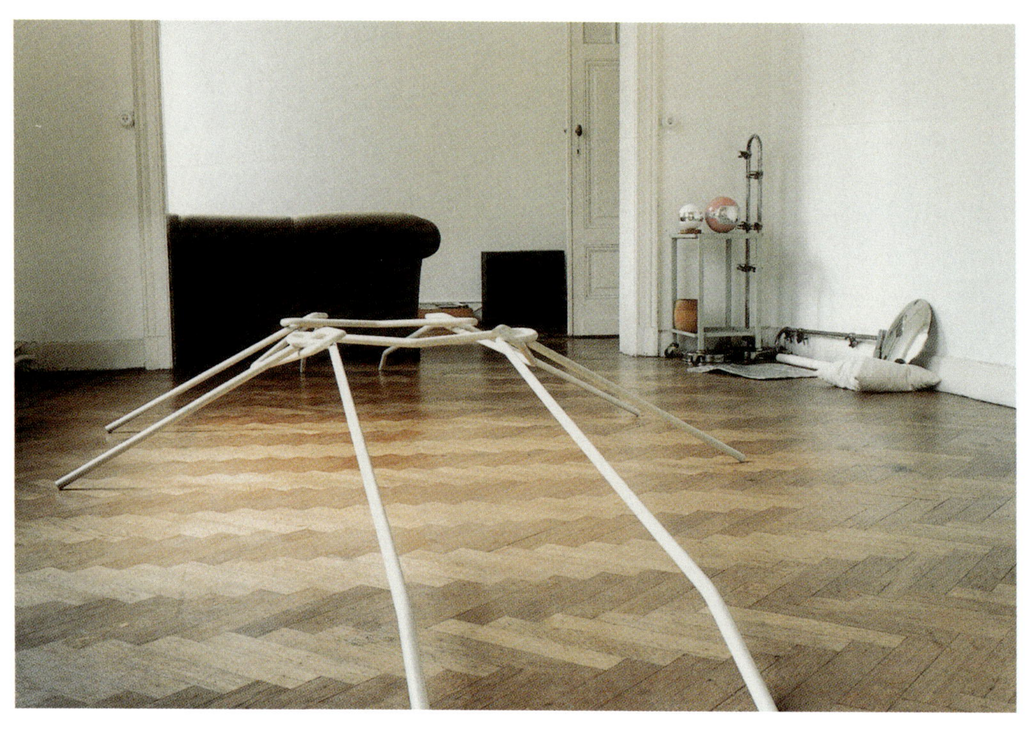

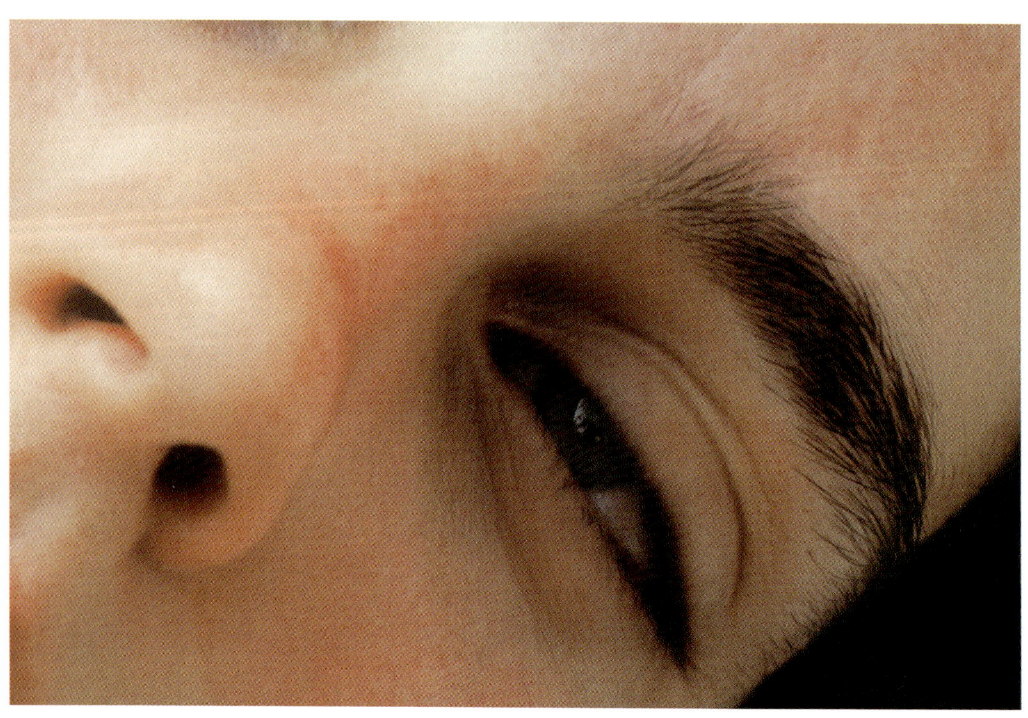

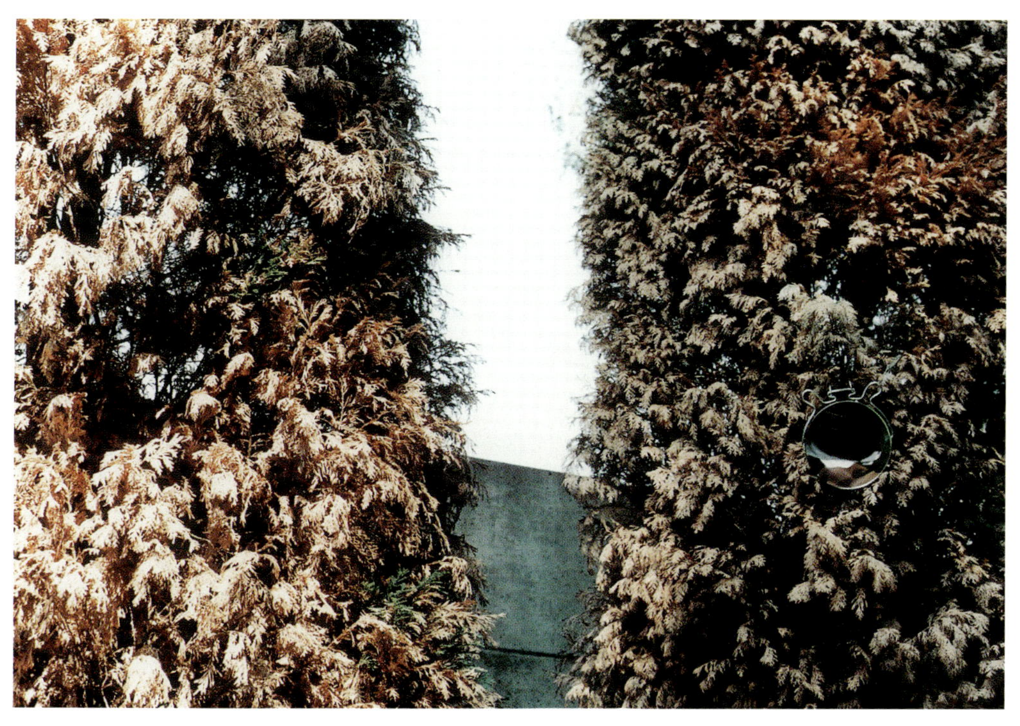

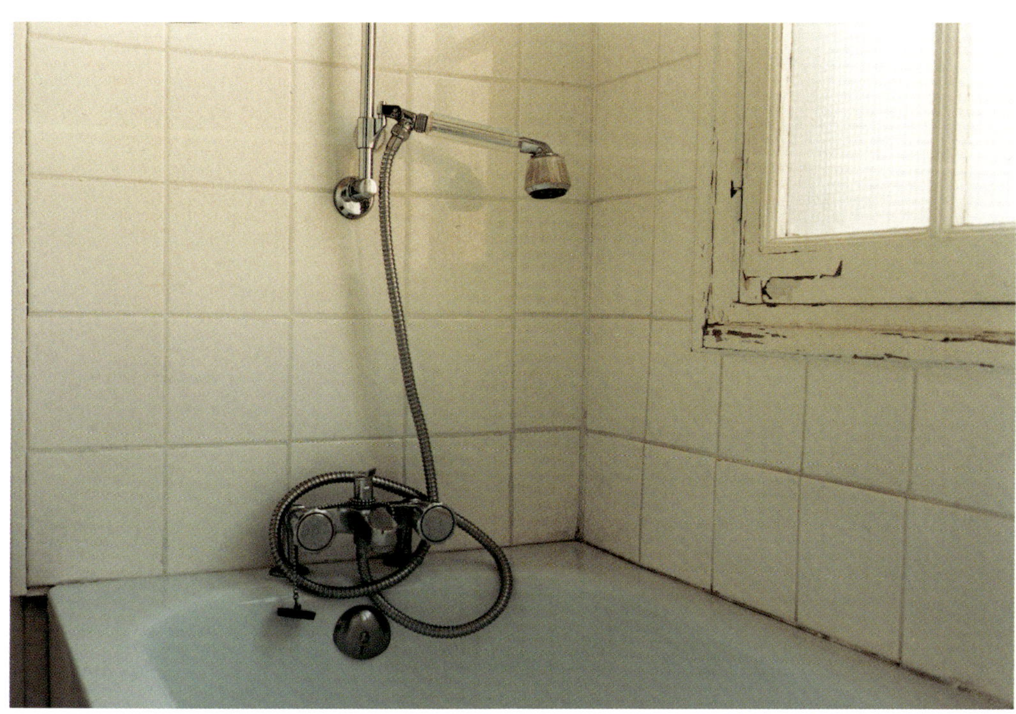

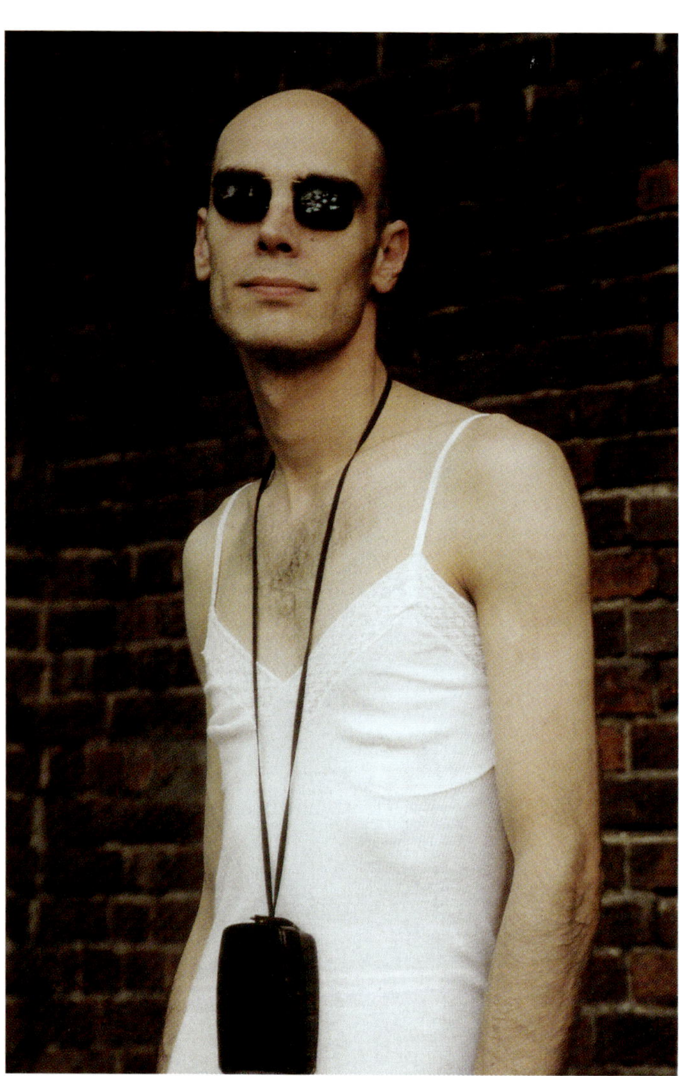

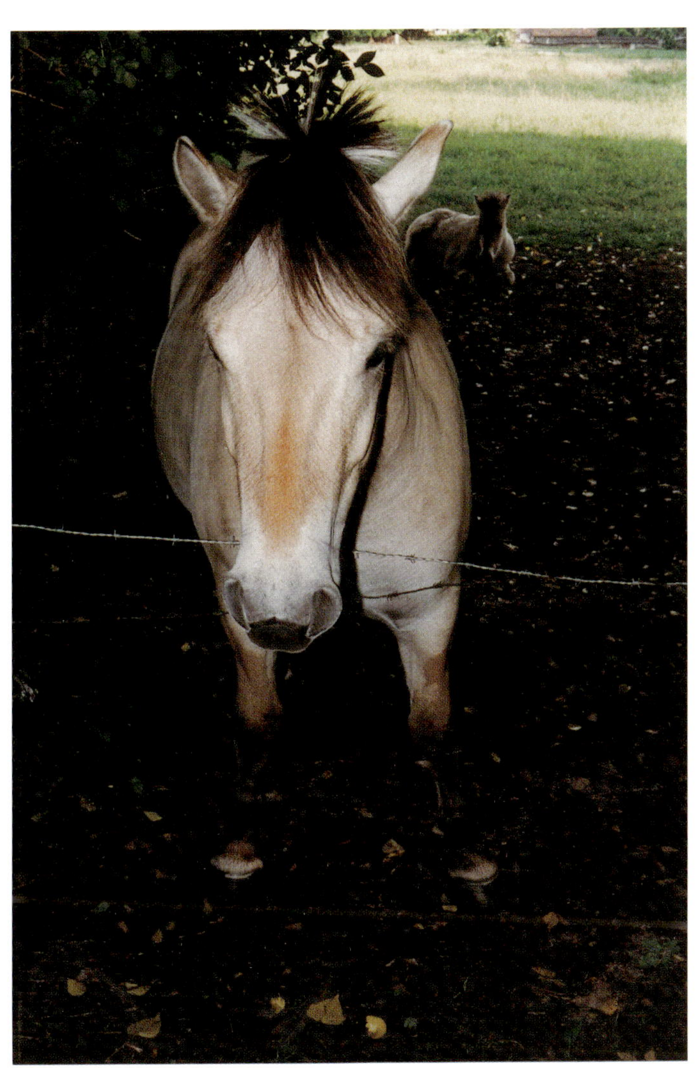

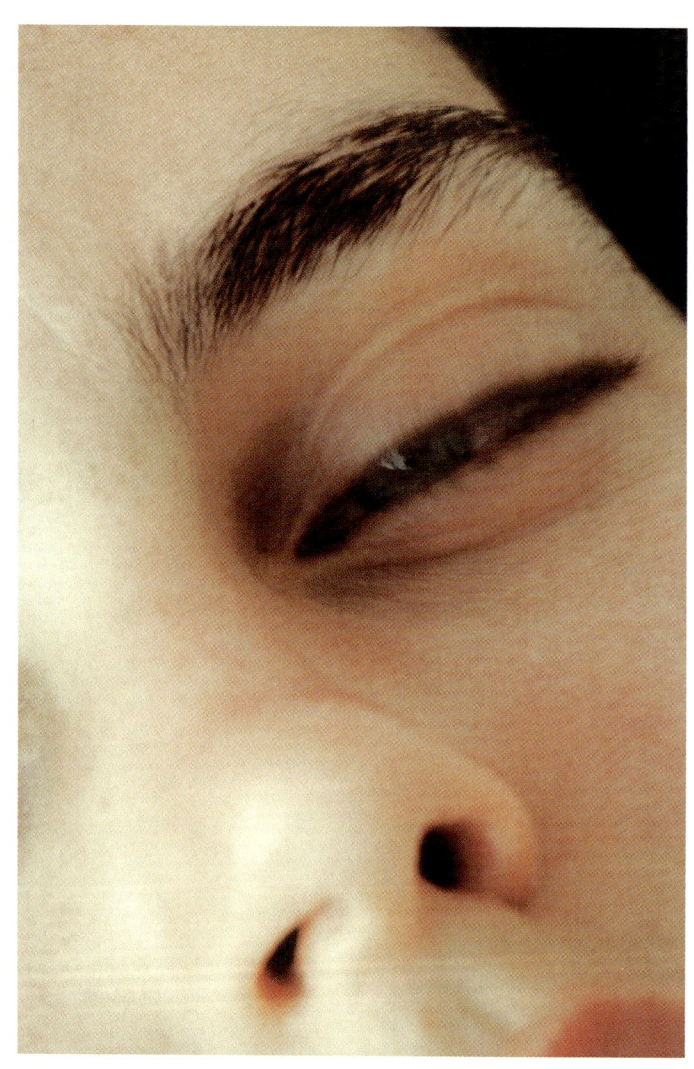

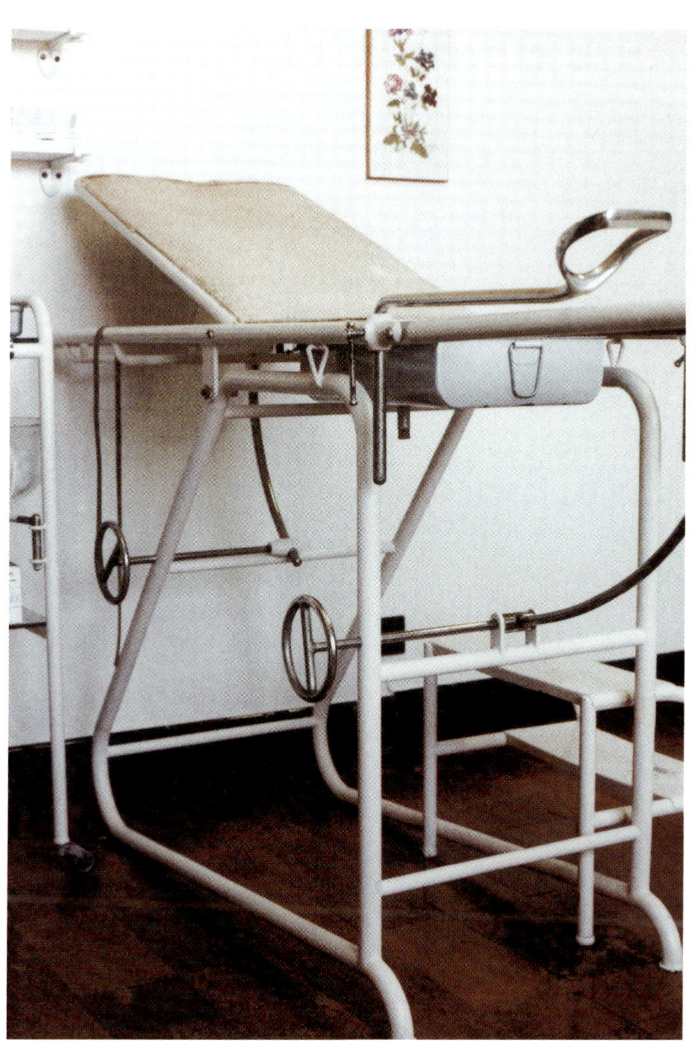

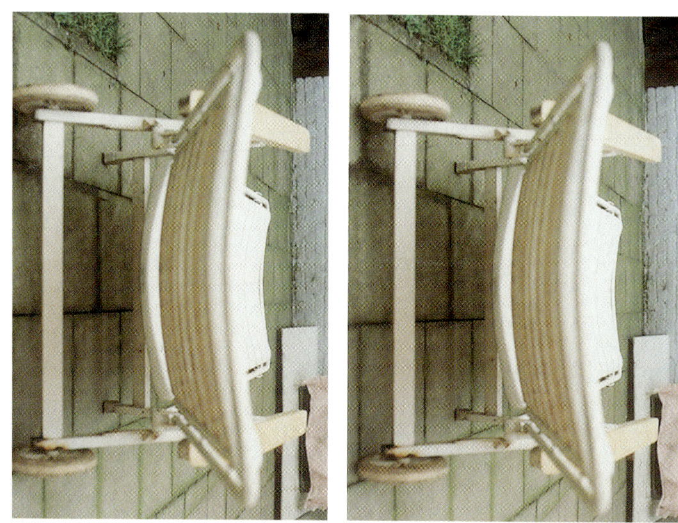

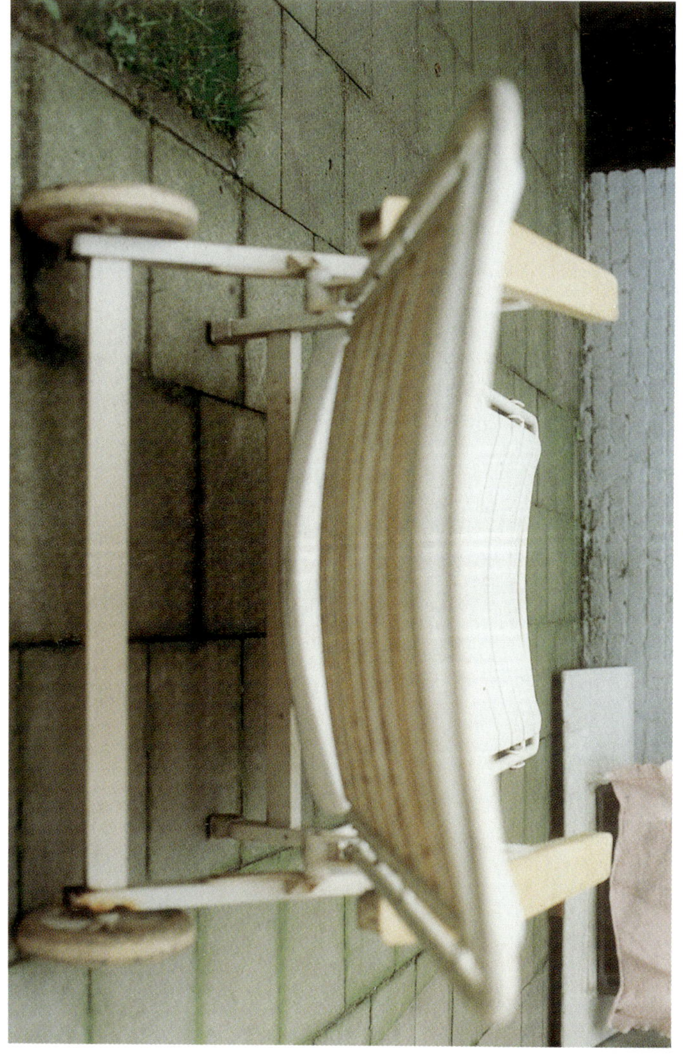

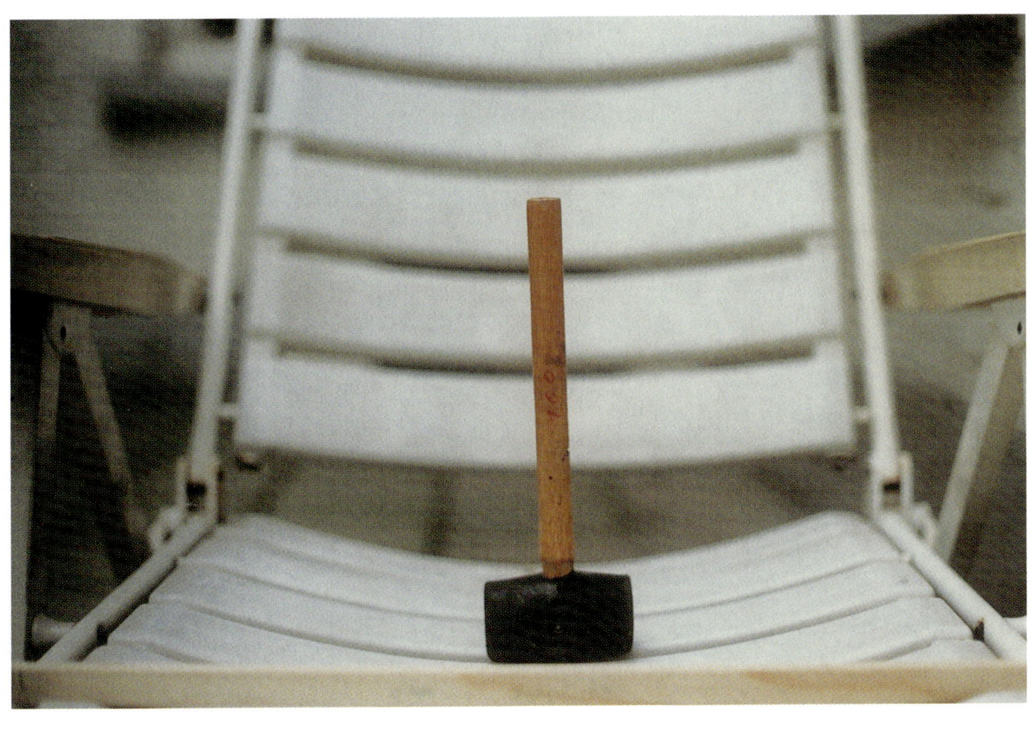

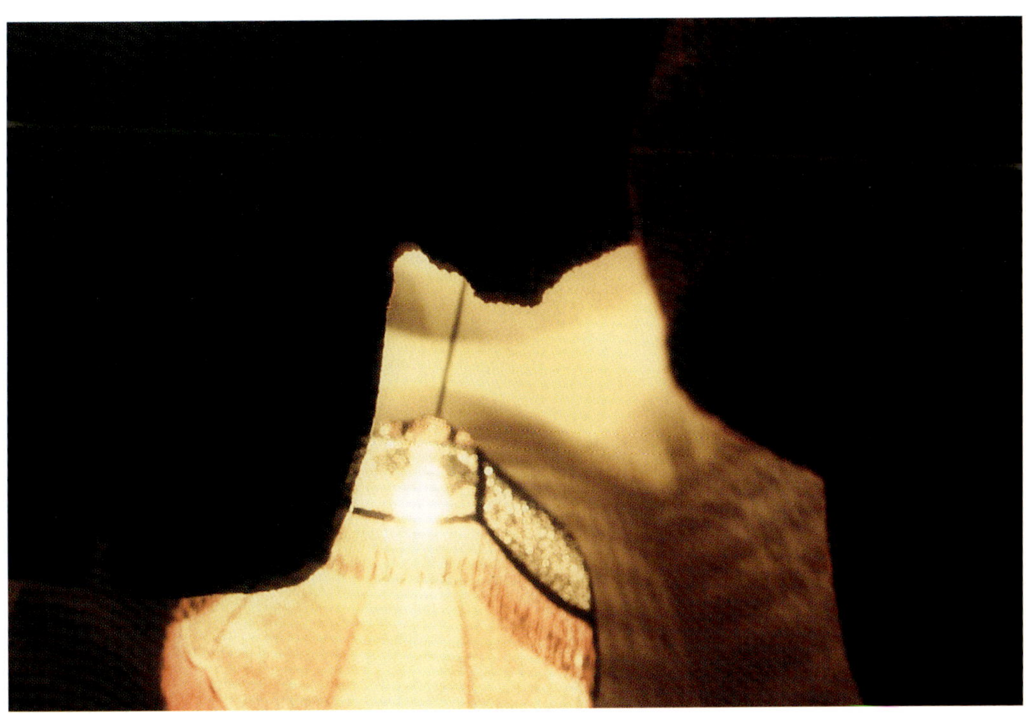

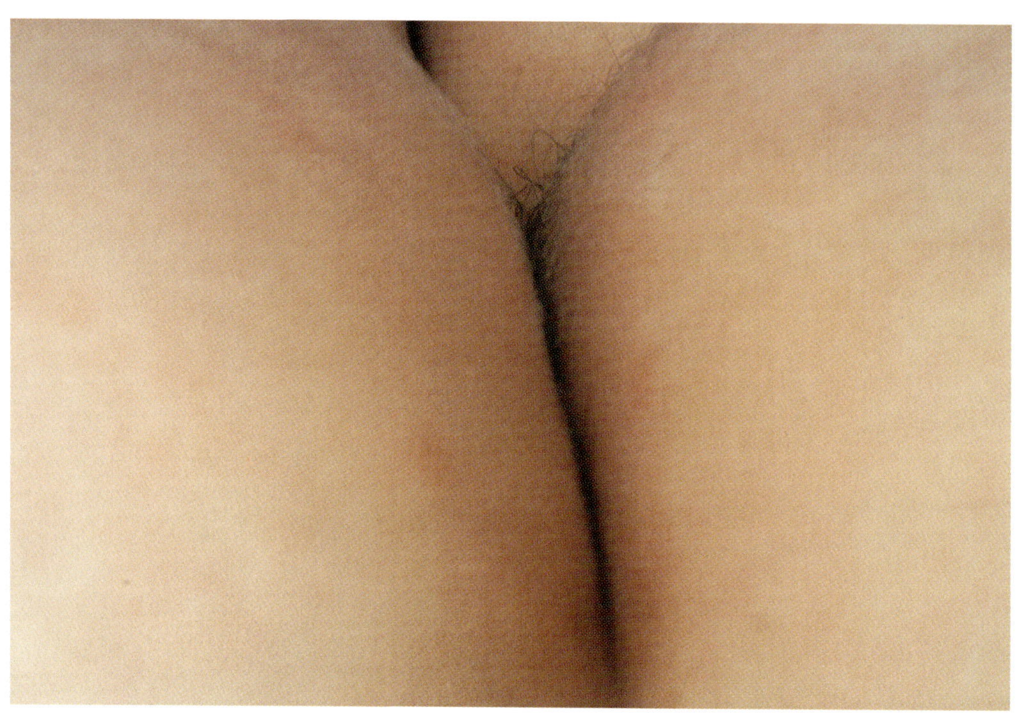

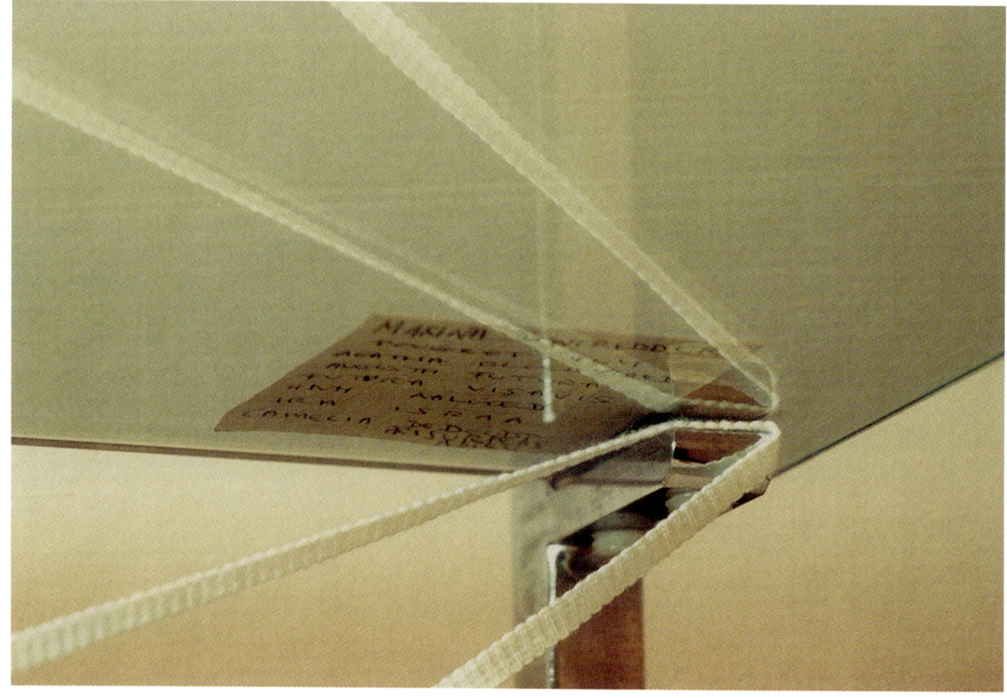

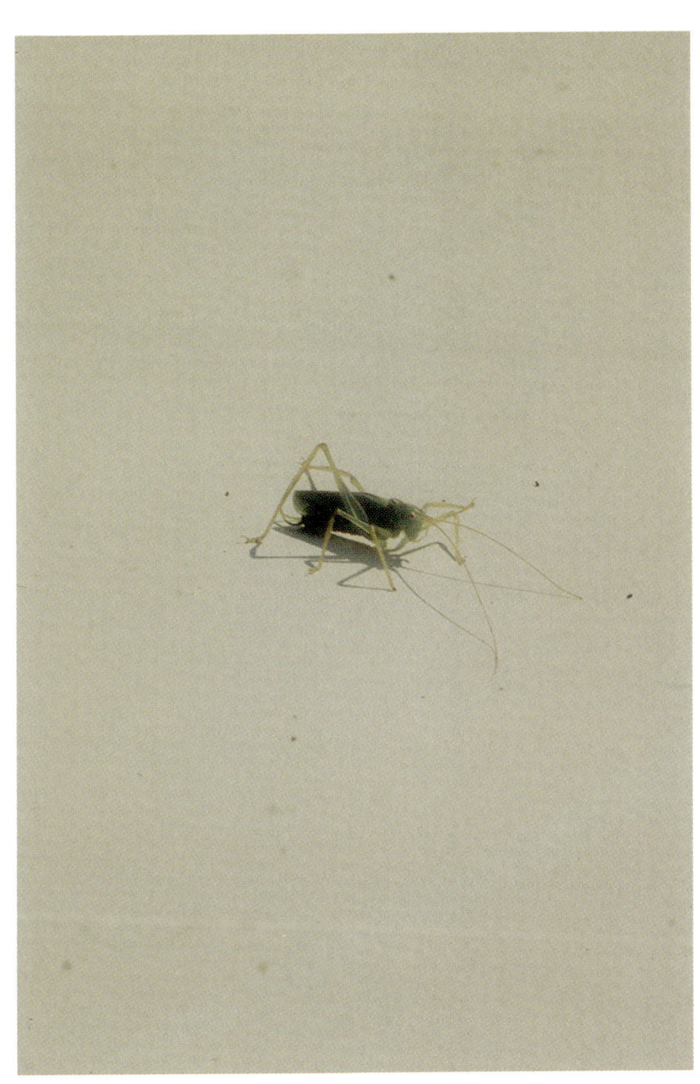

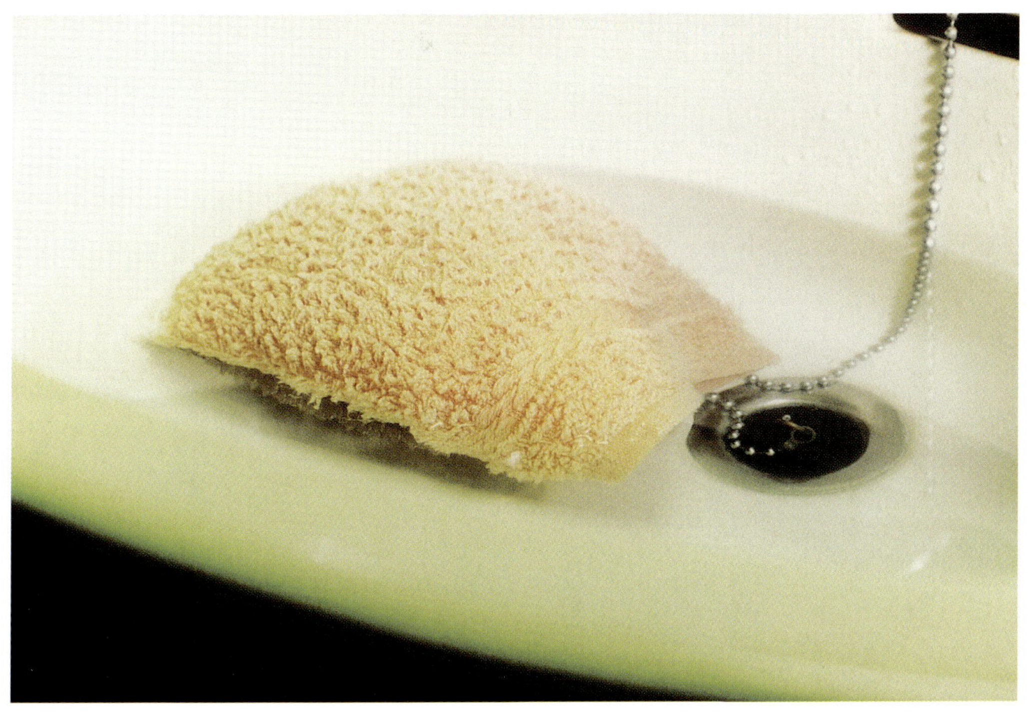

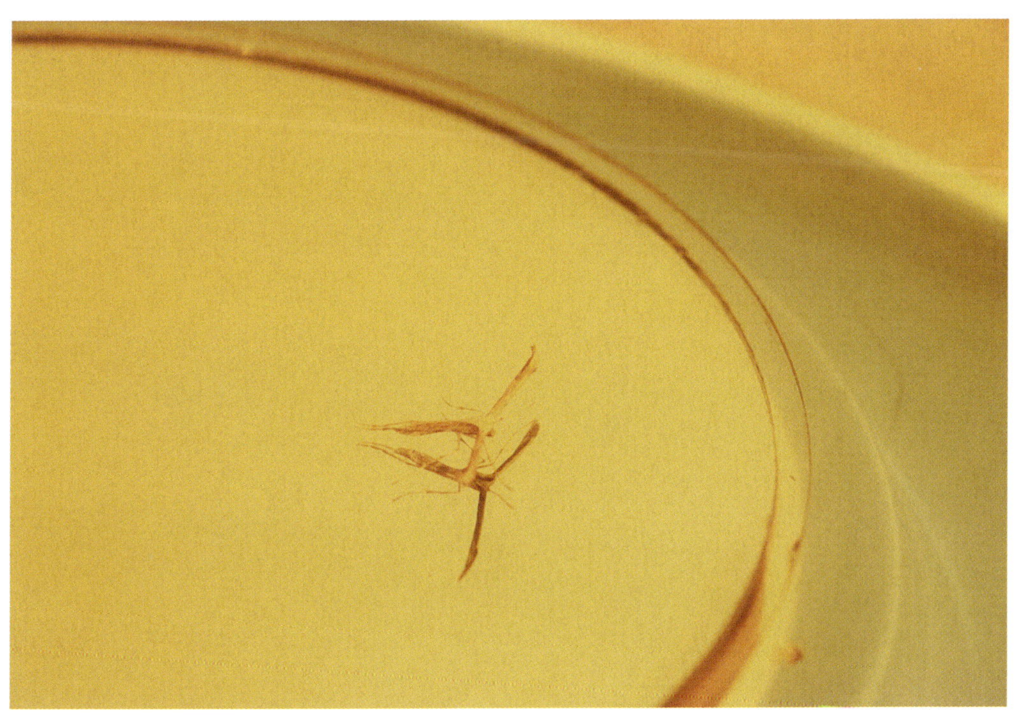

*

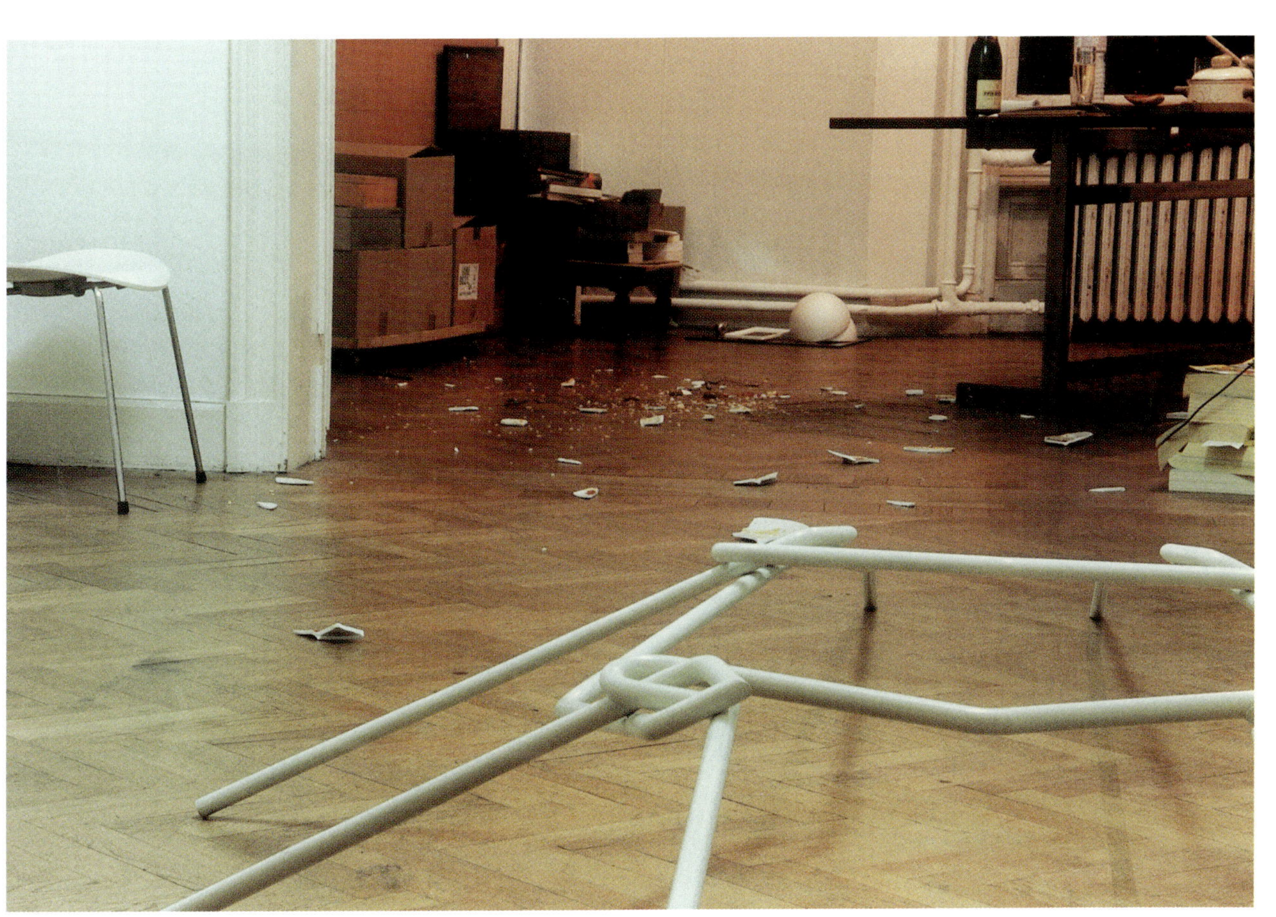

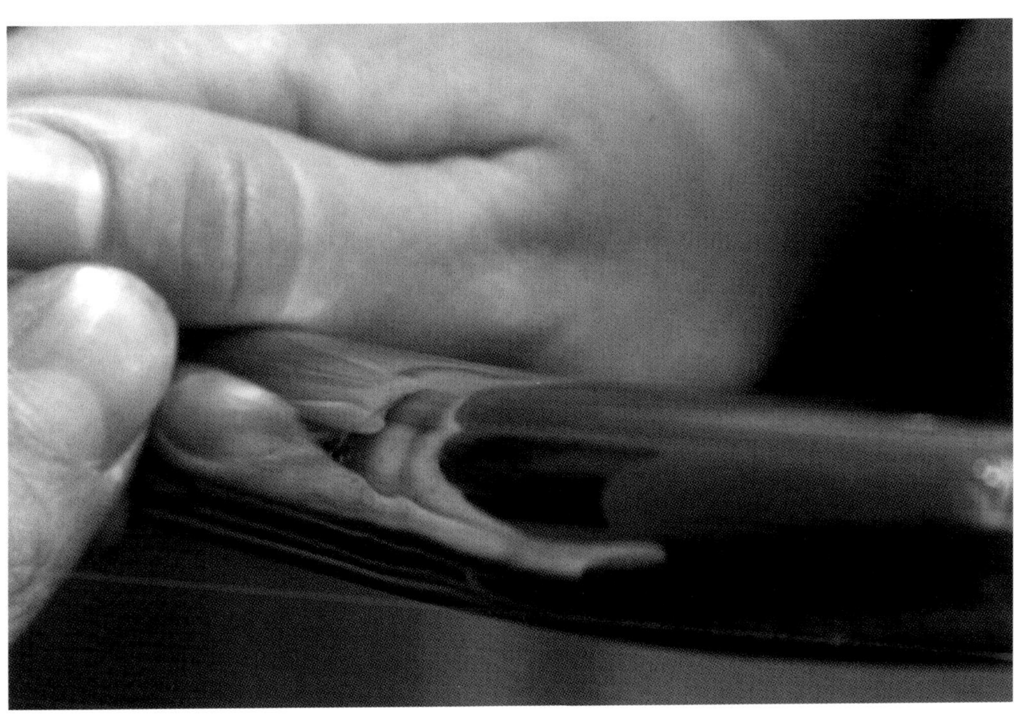

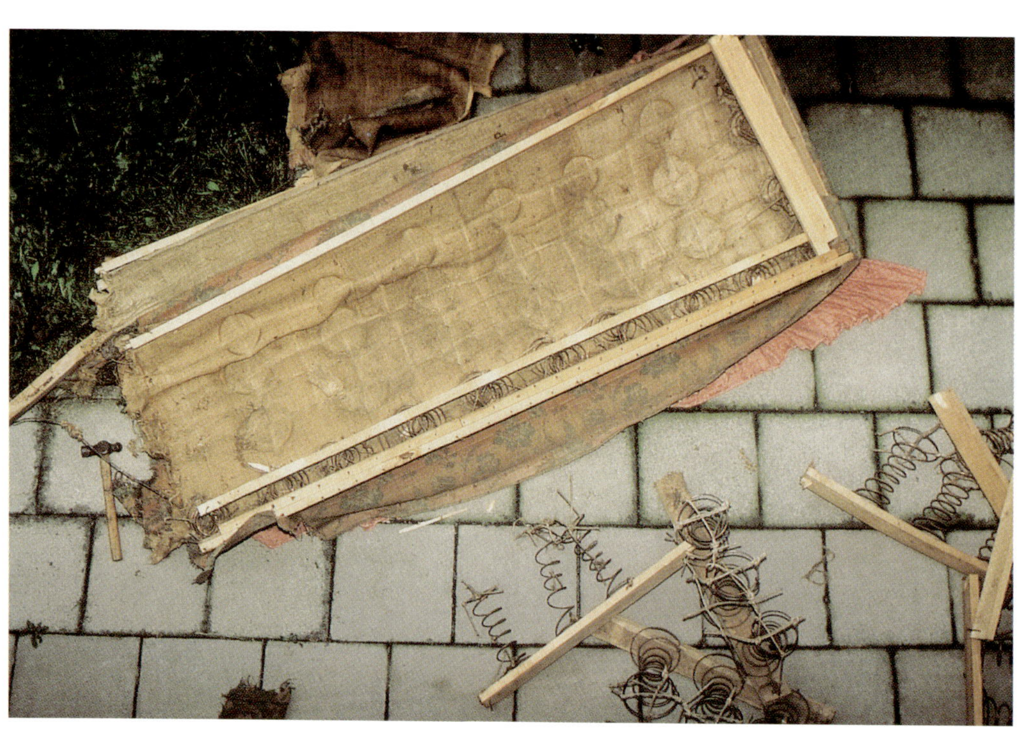

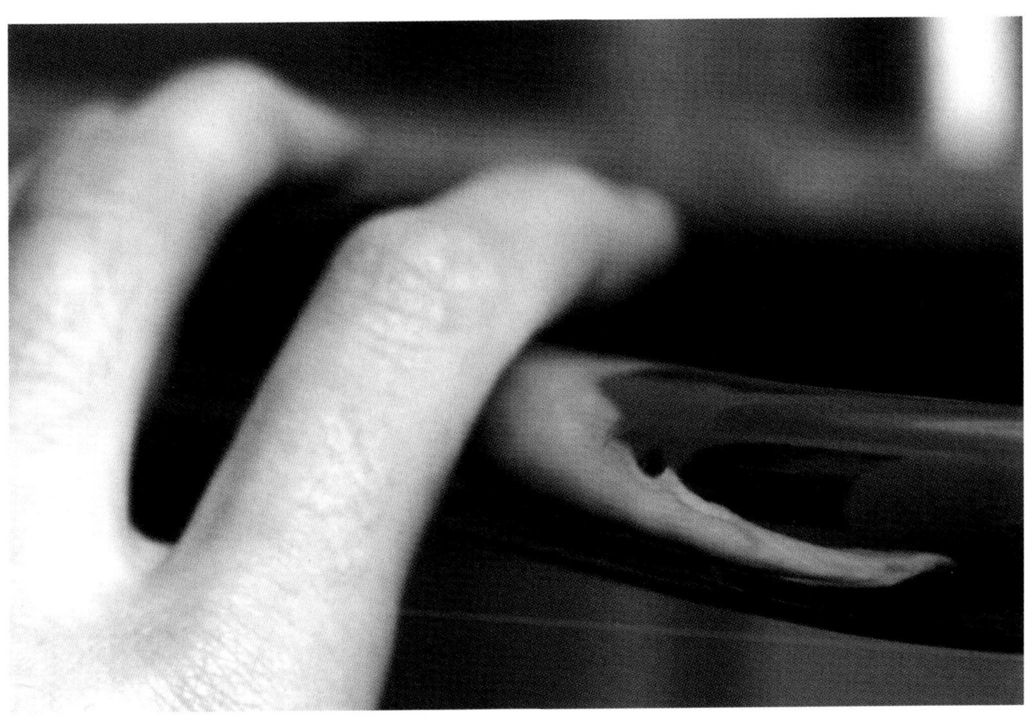

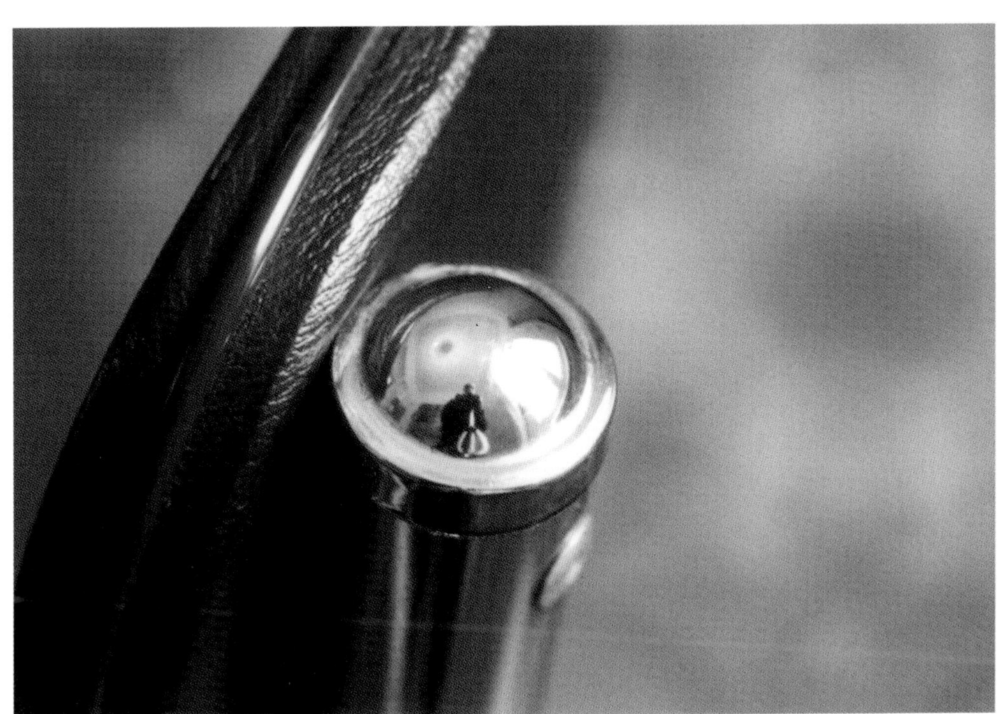

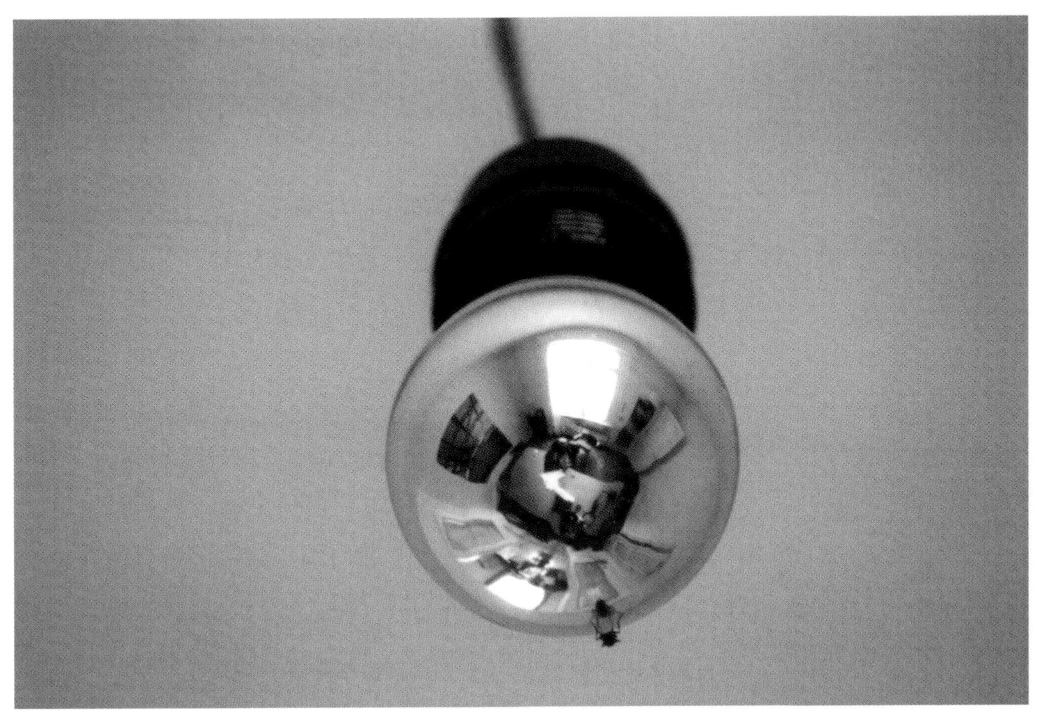

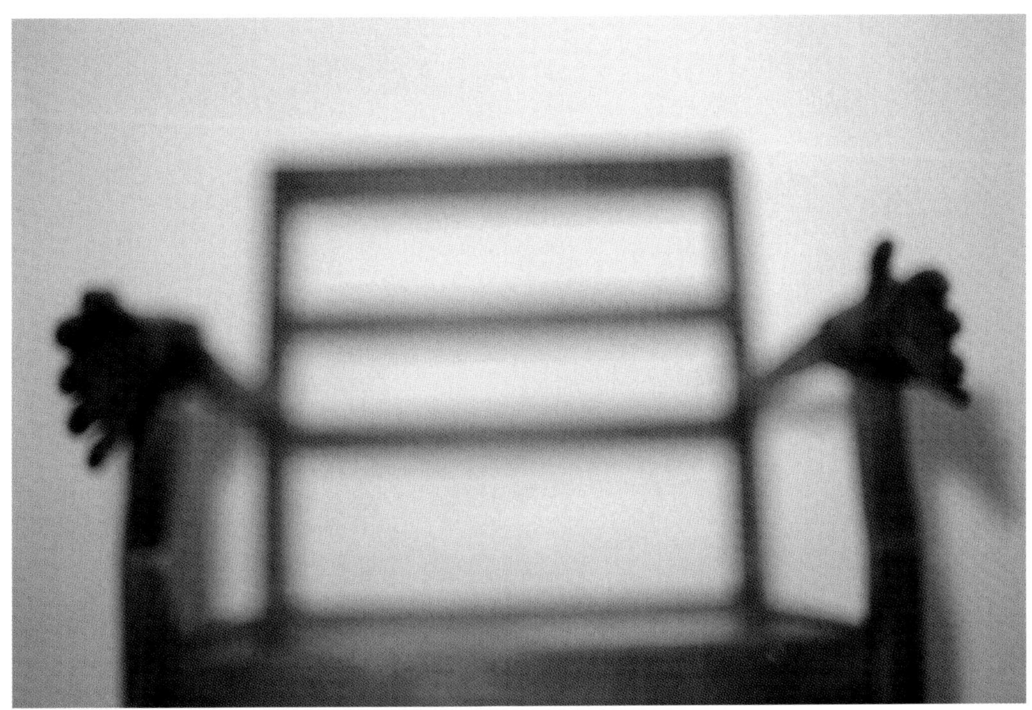

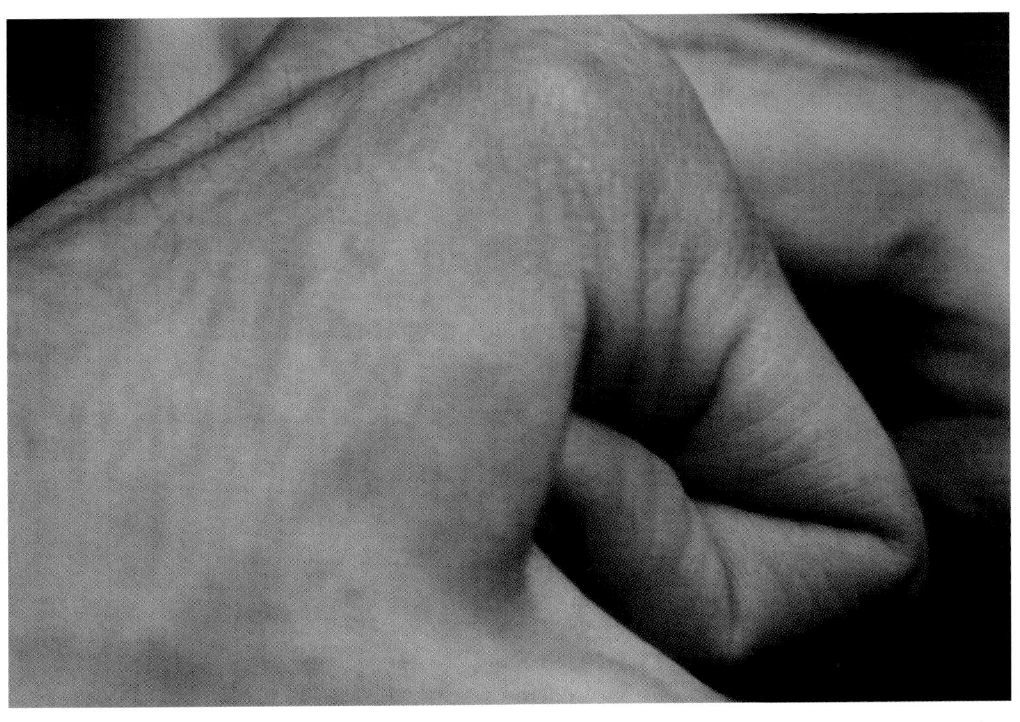

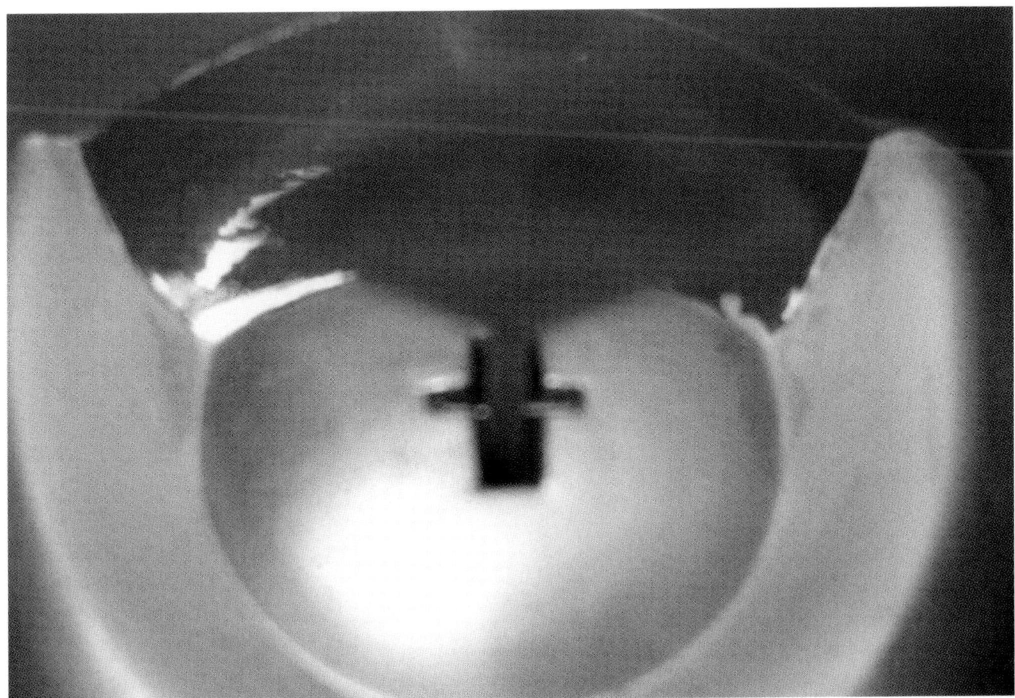

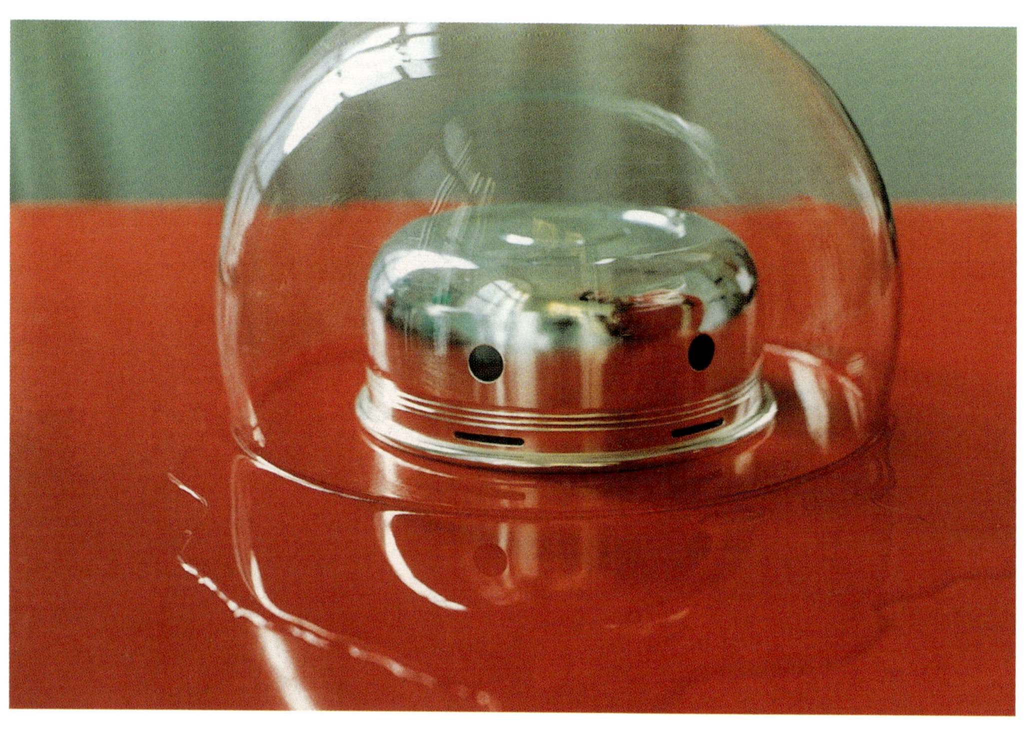

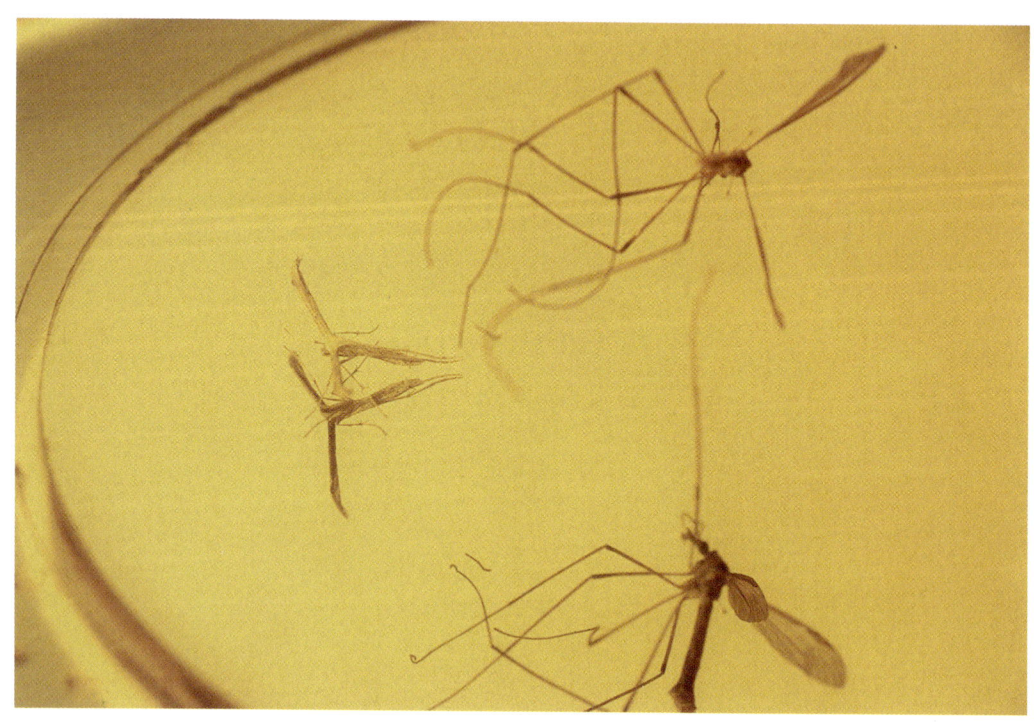

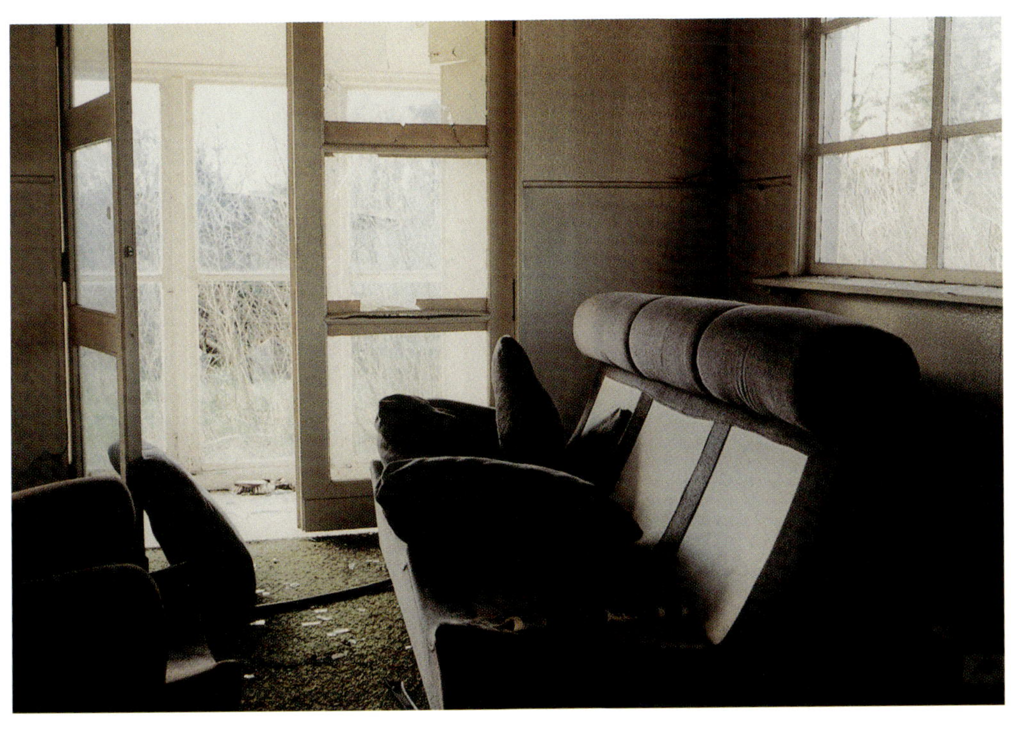

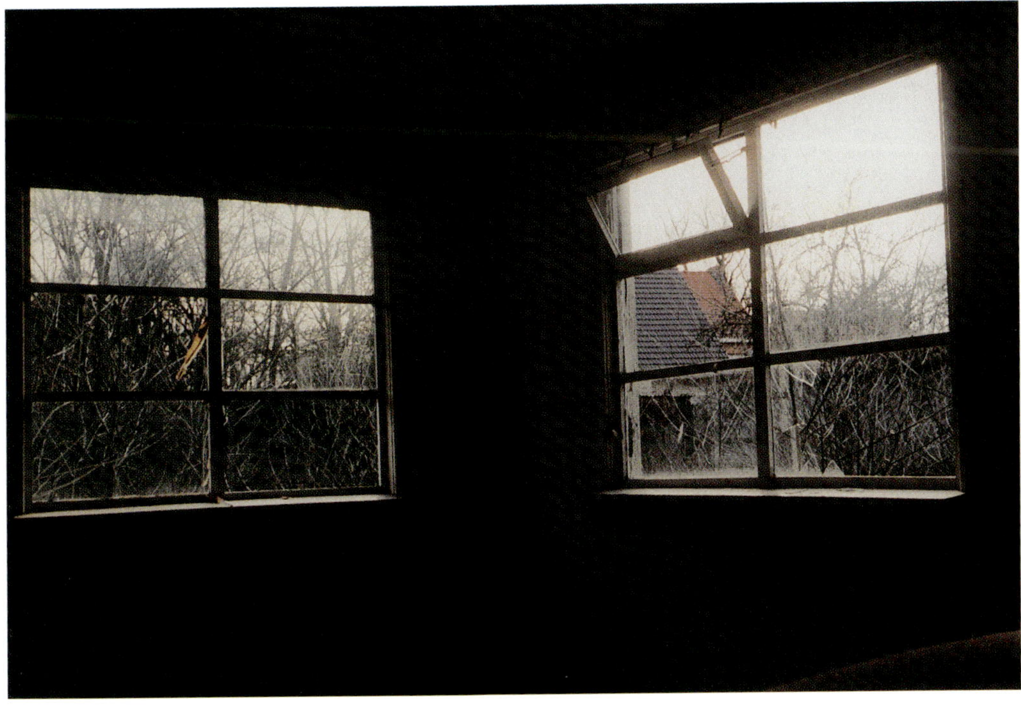

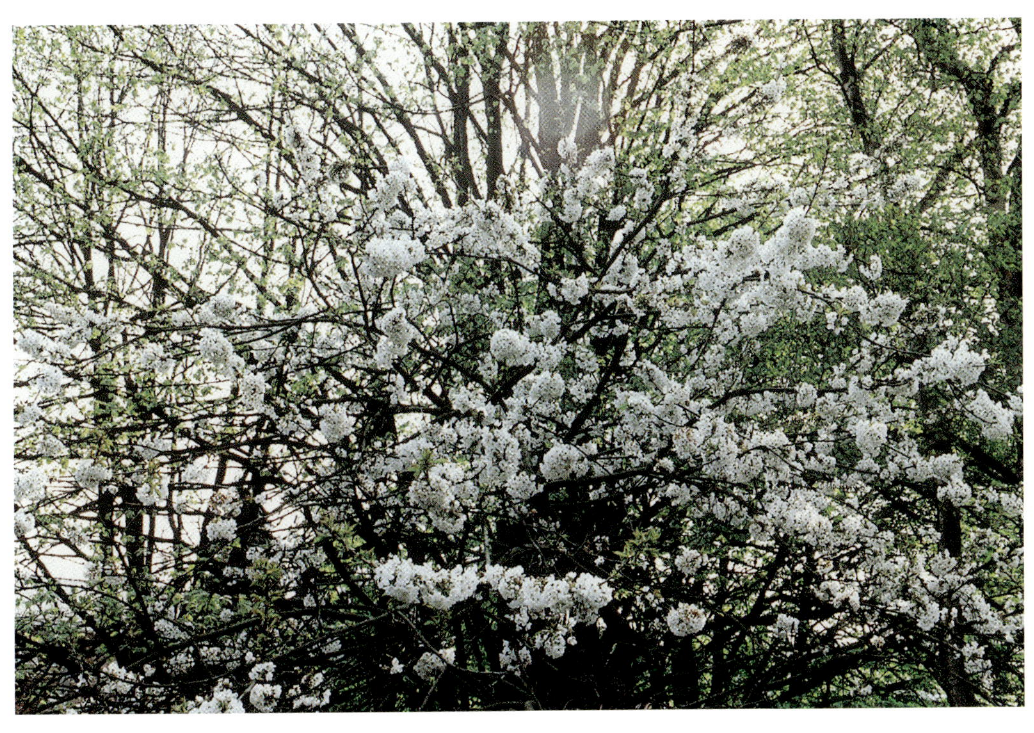

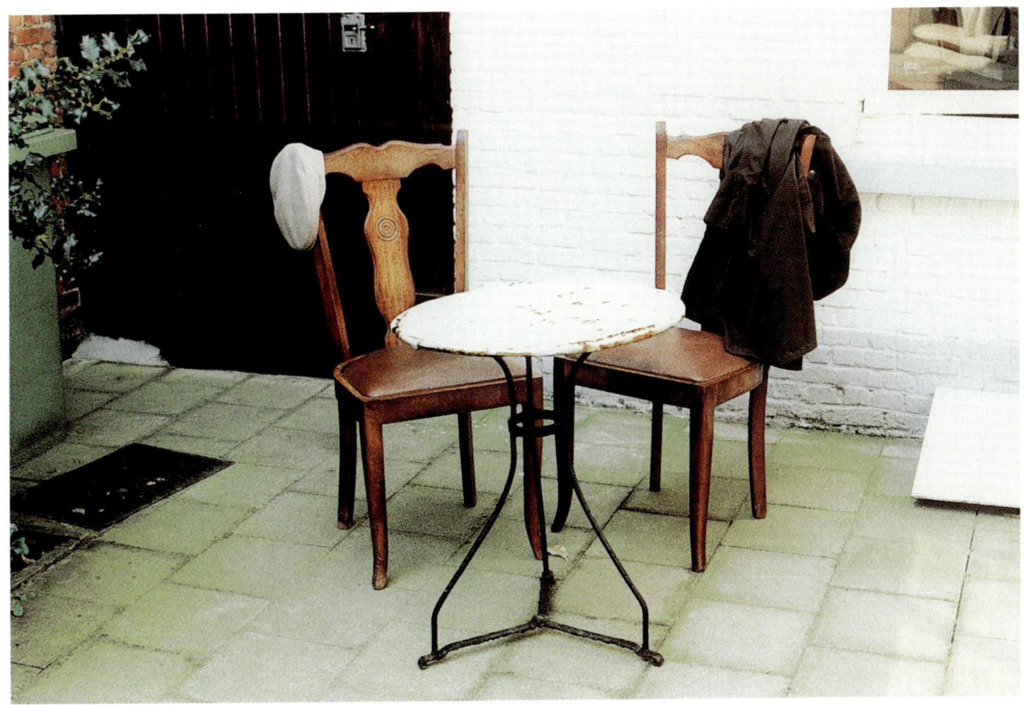

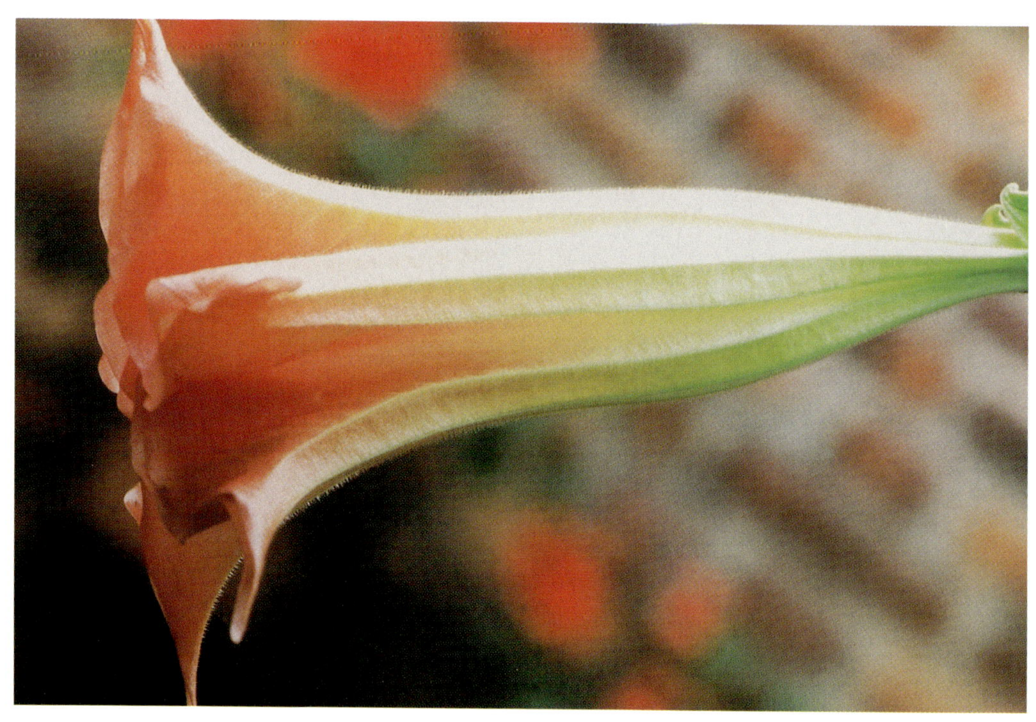

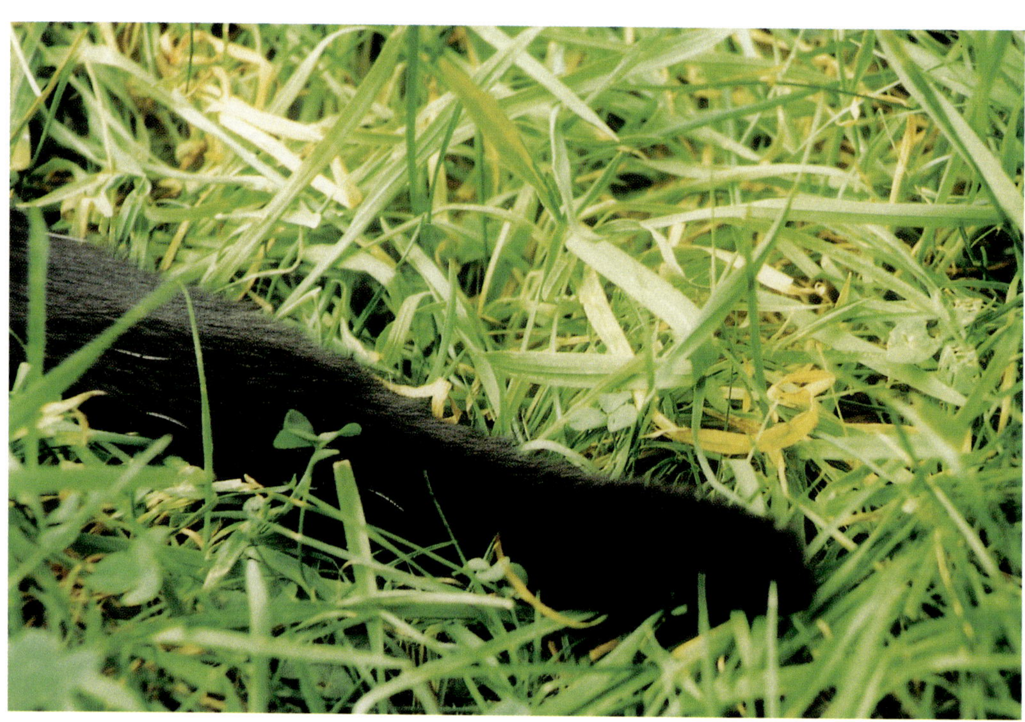

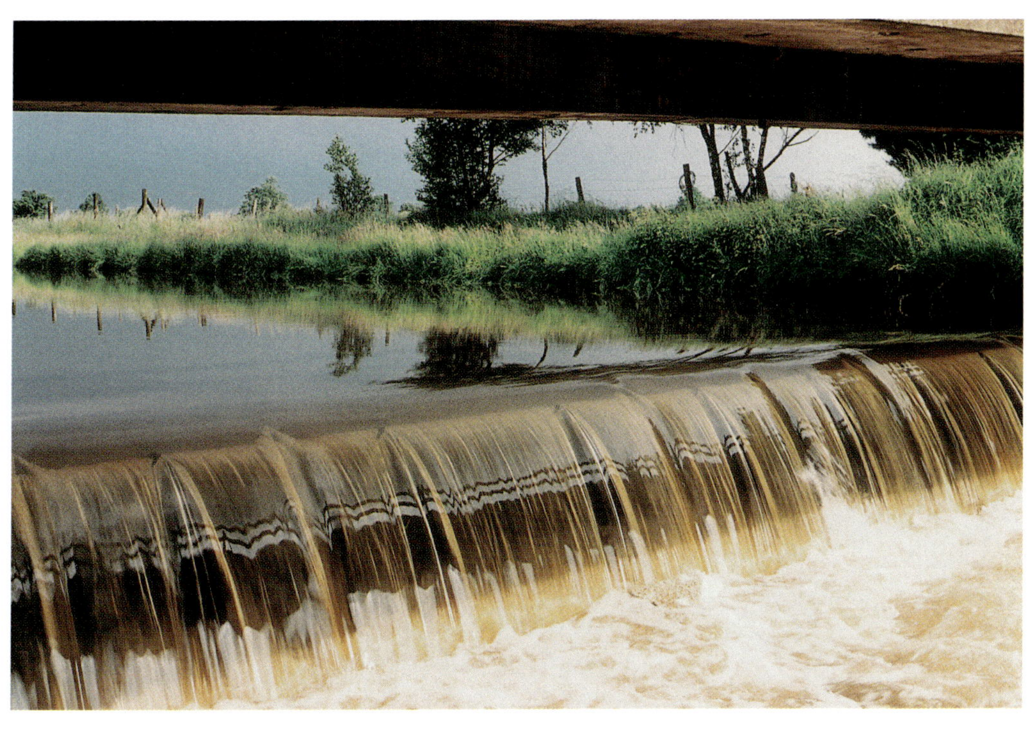

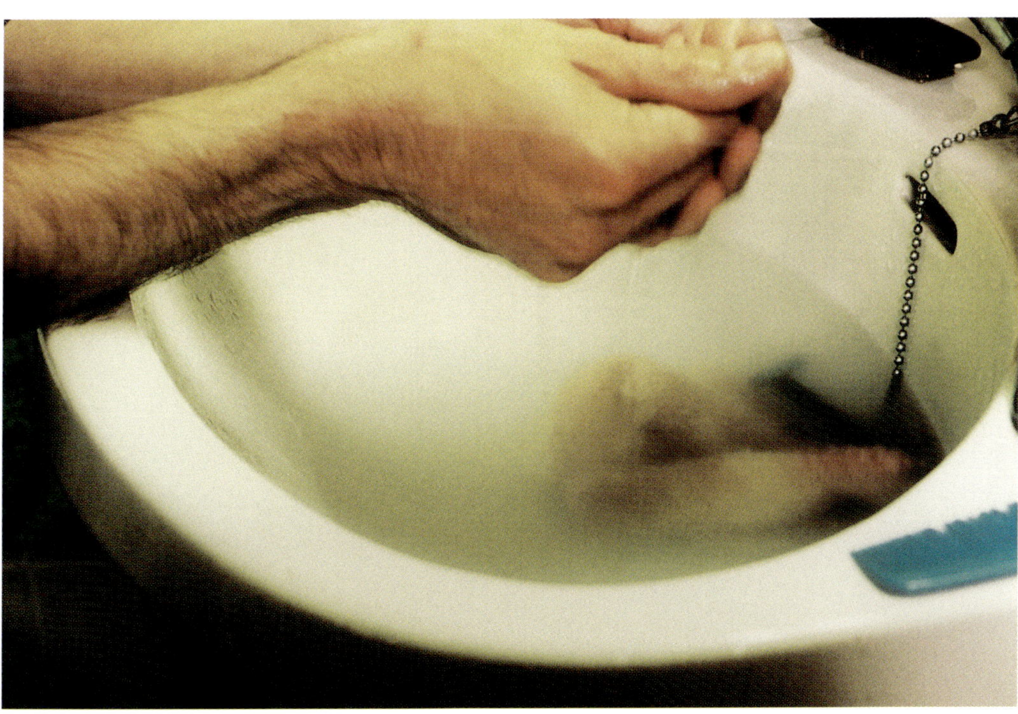

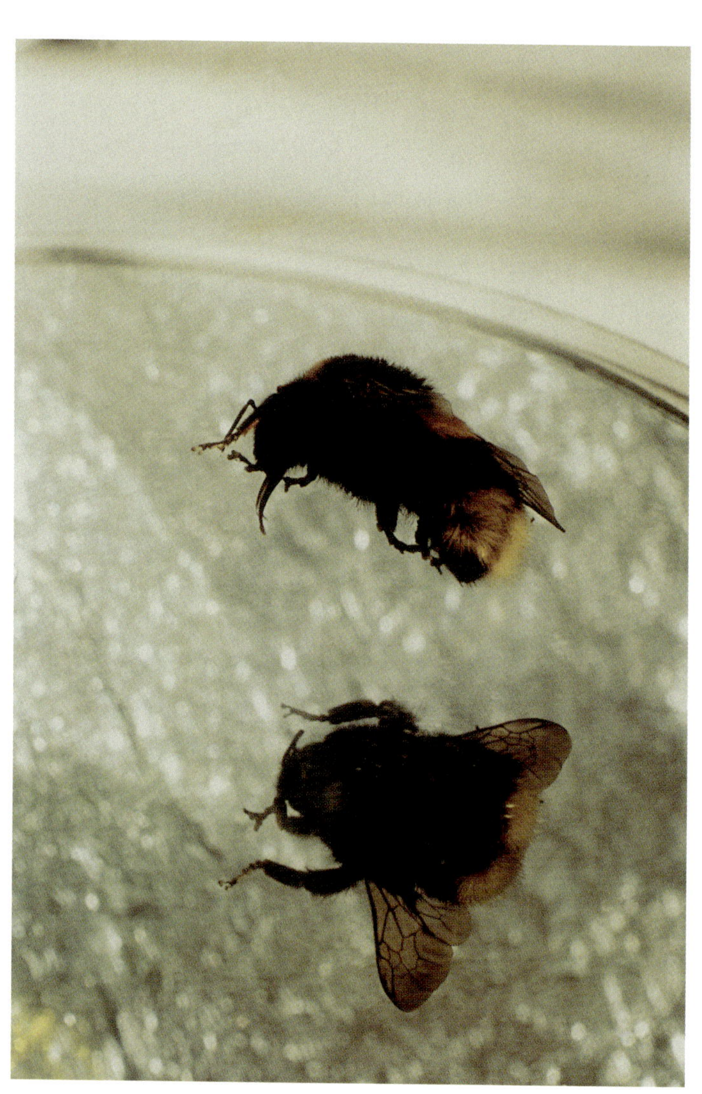

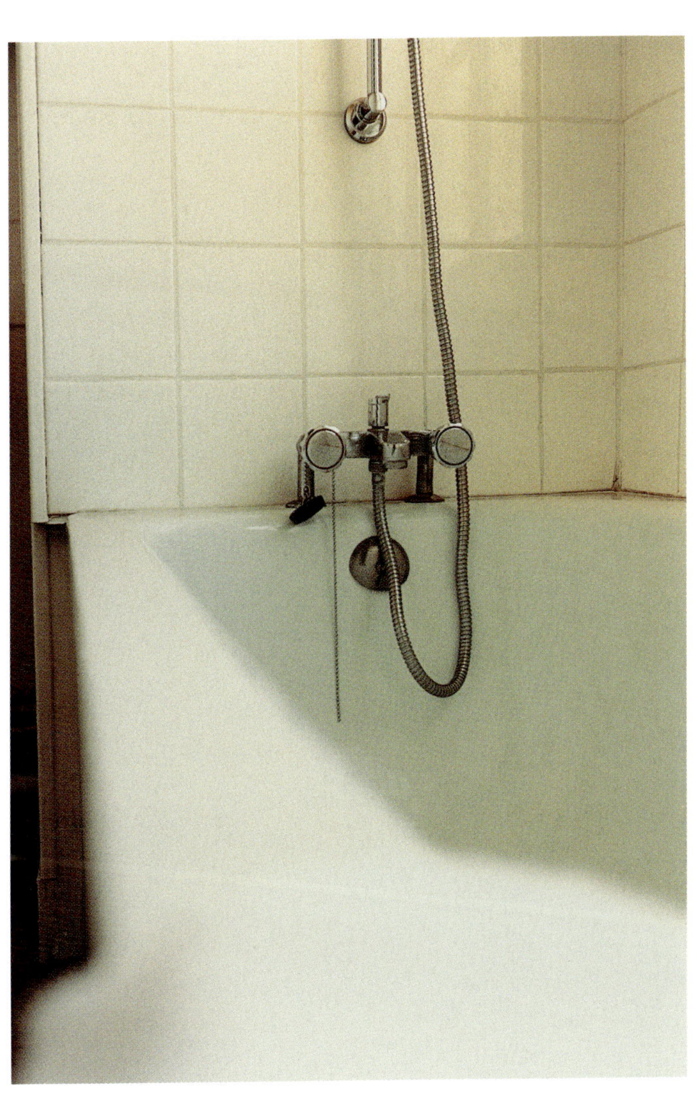

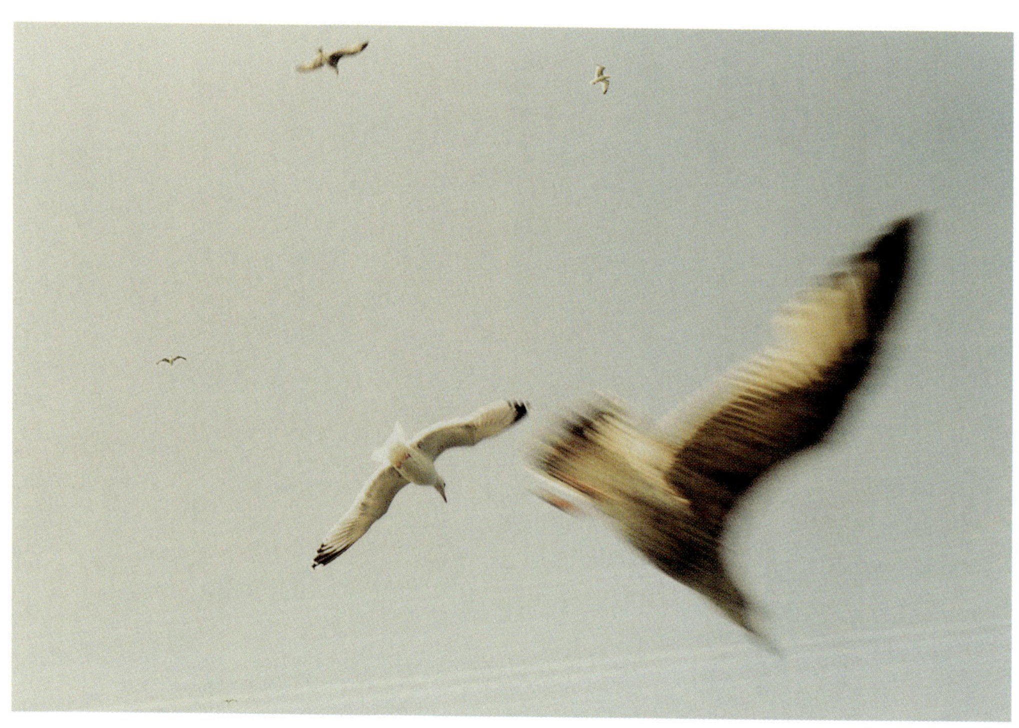

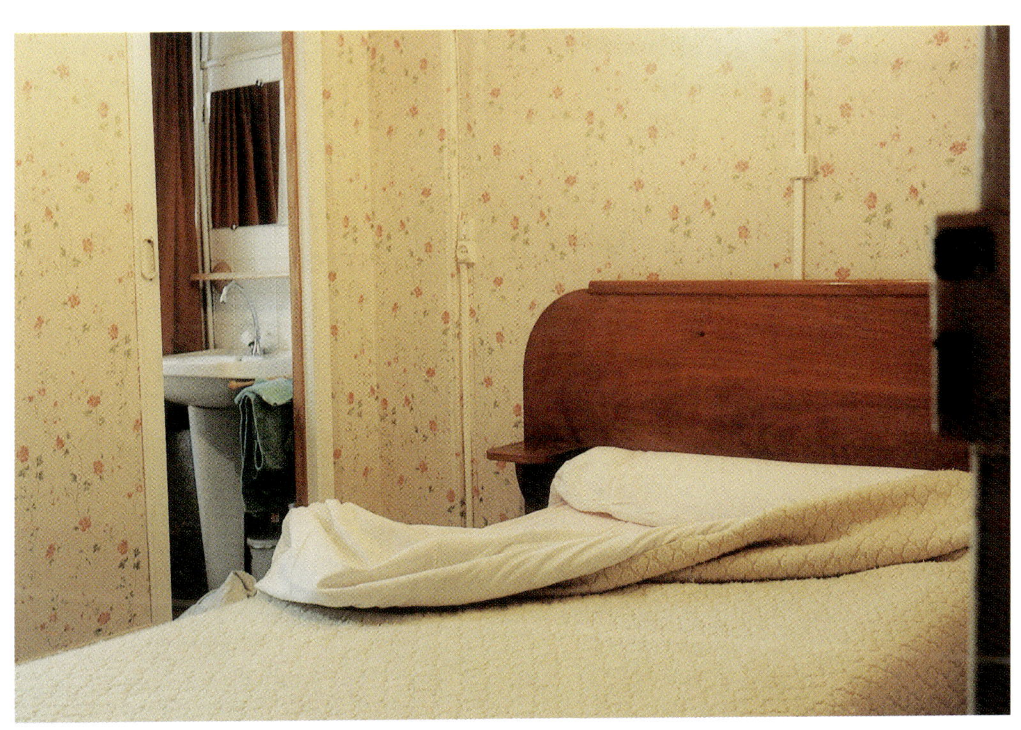

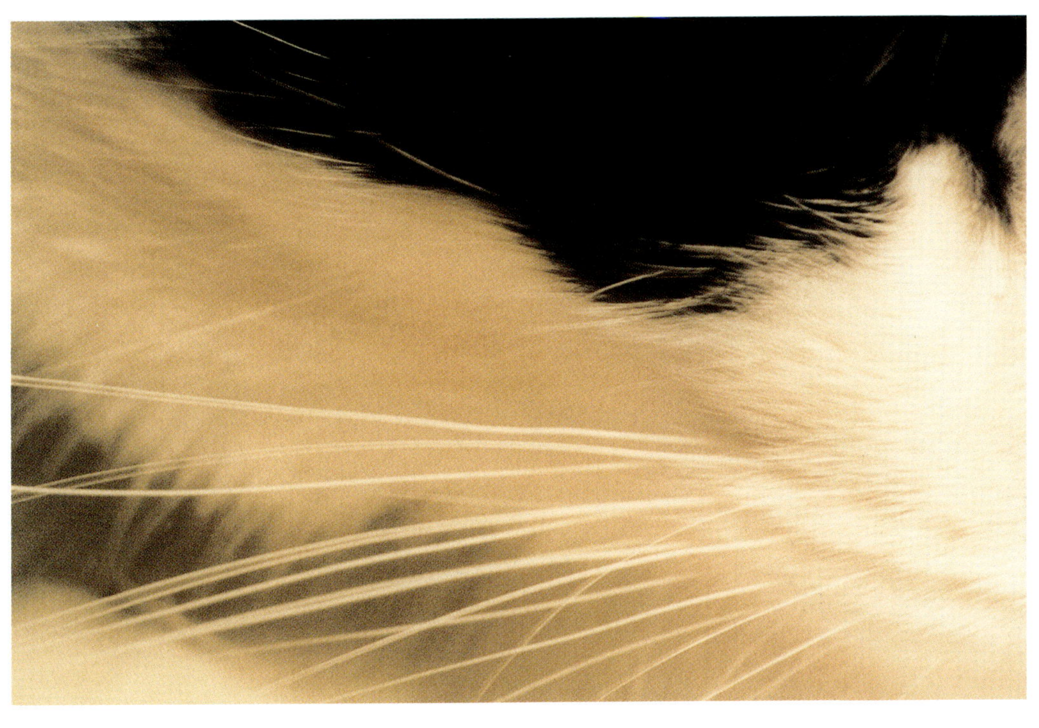

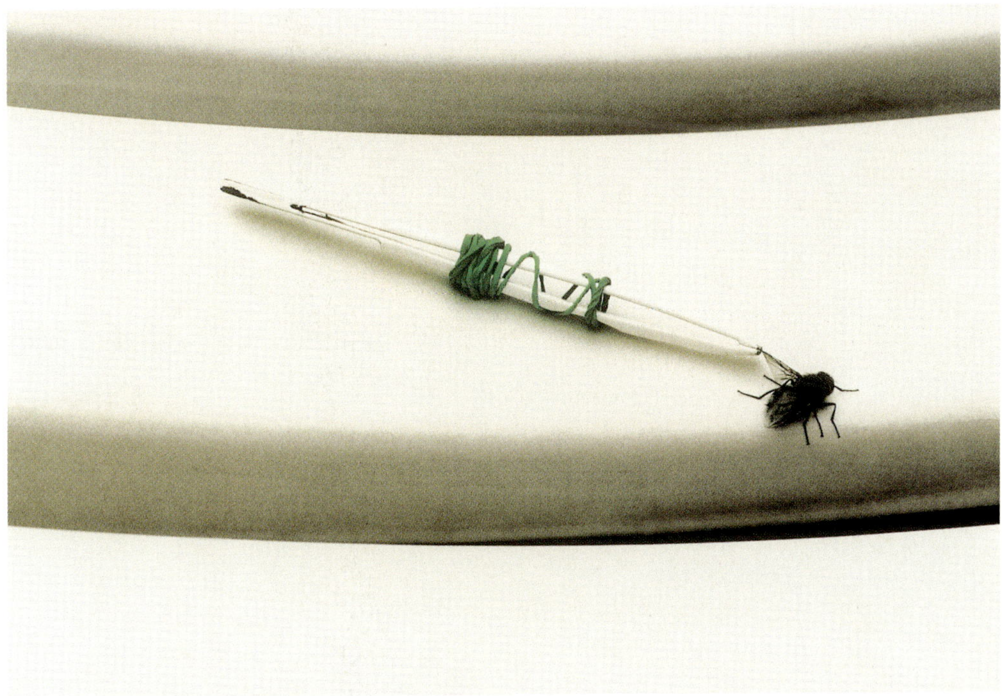

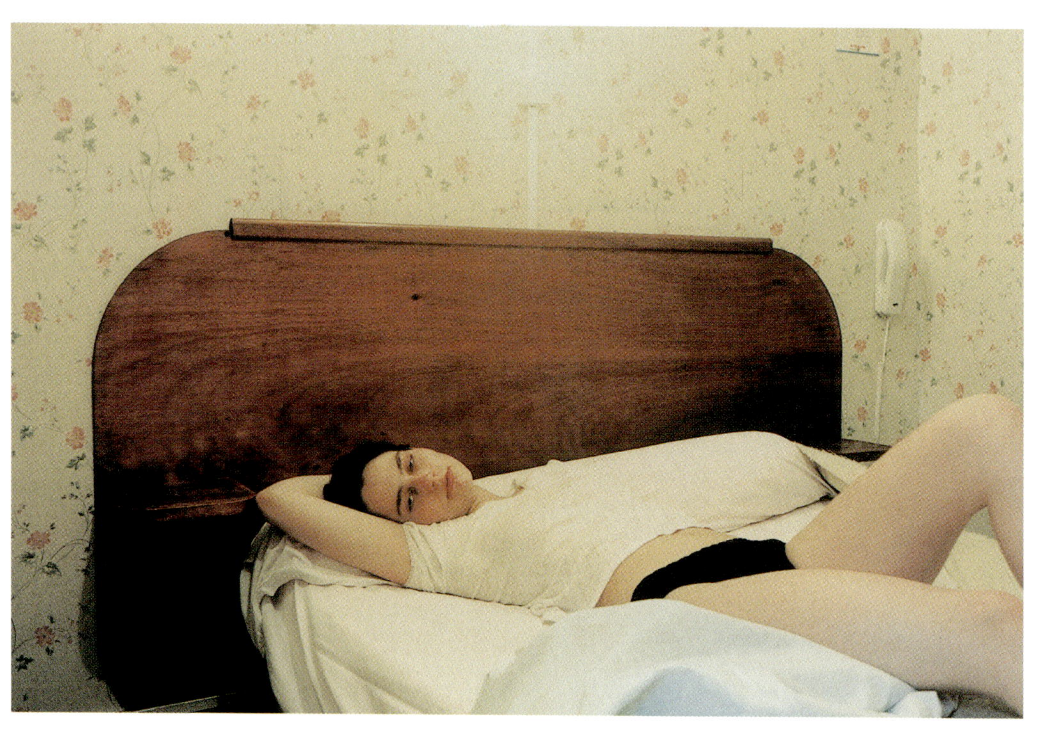

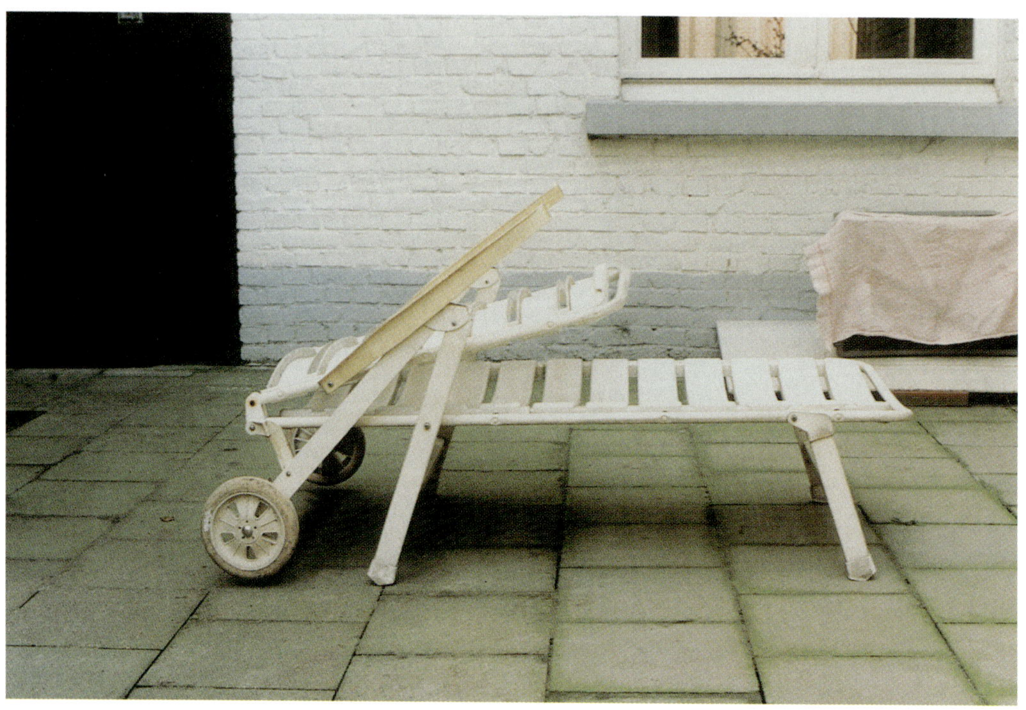

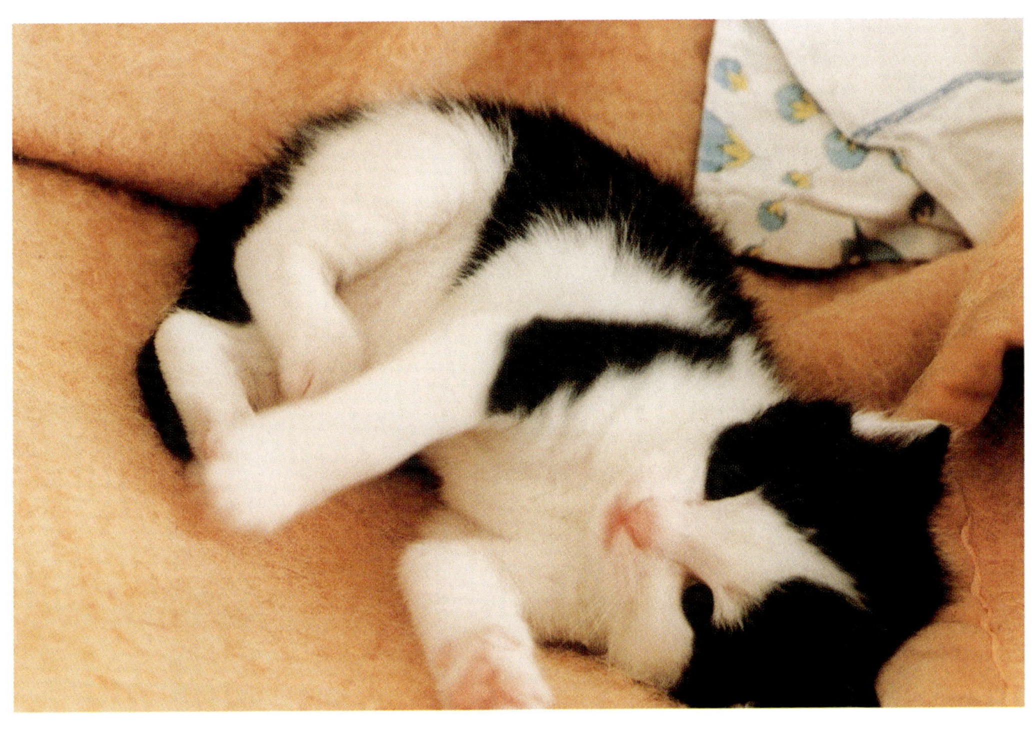

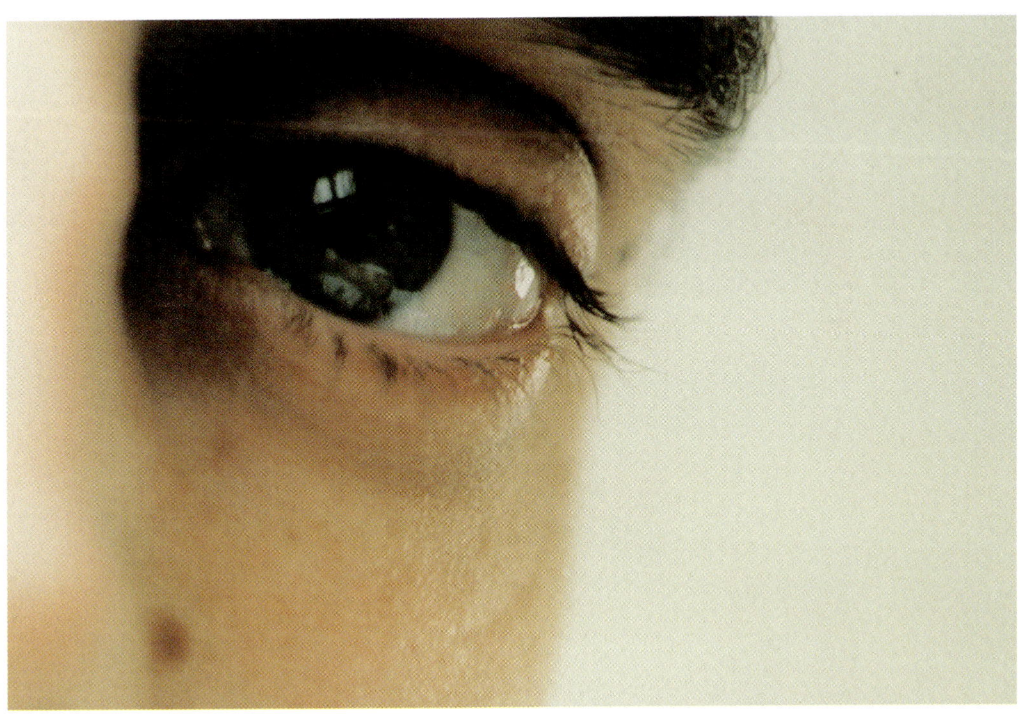

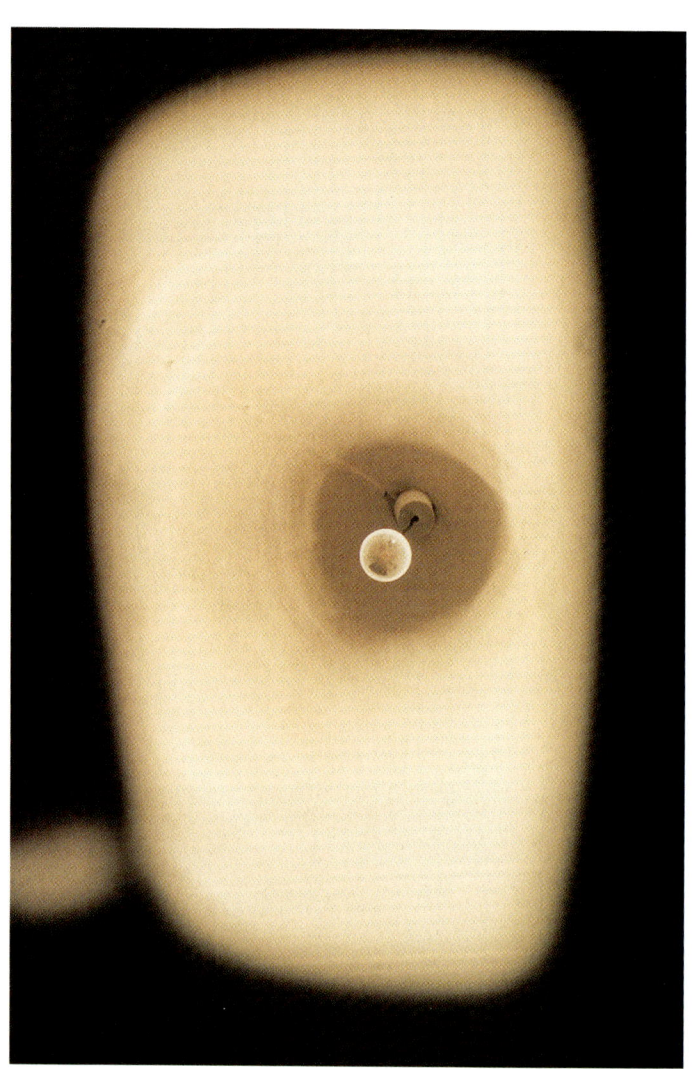

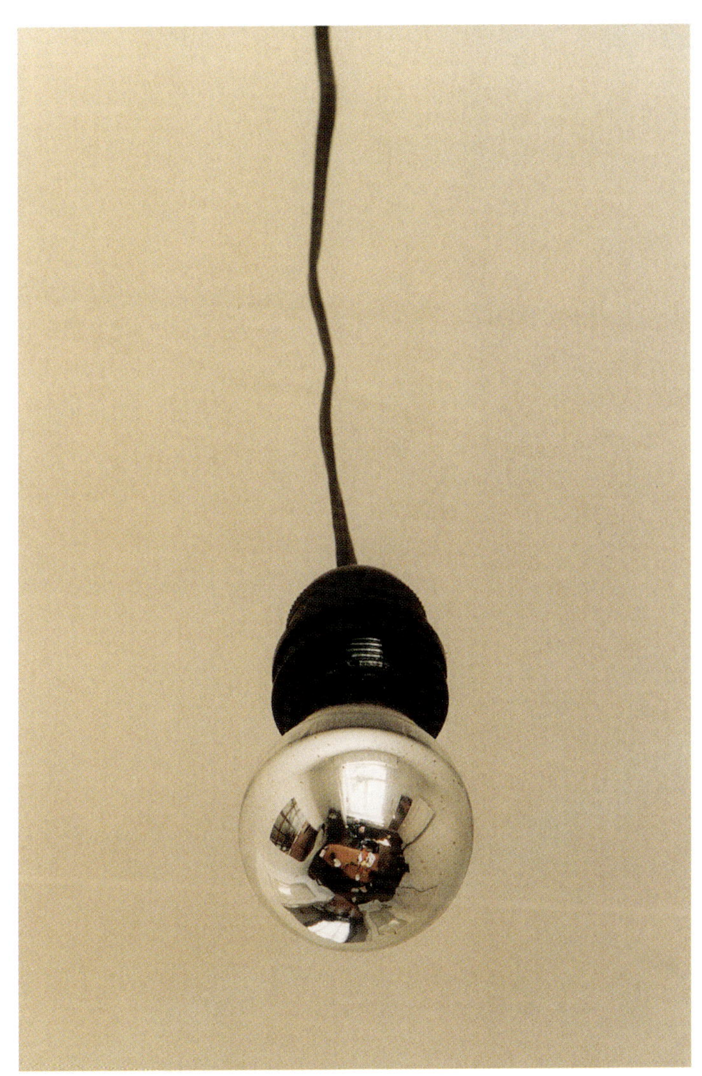

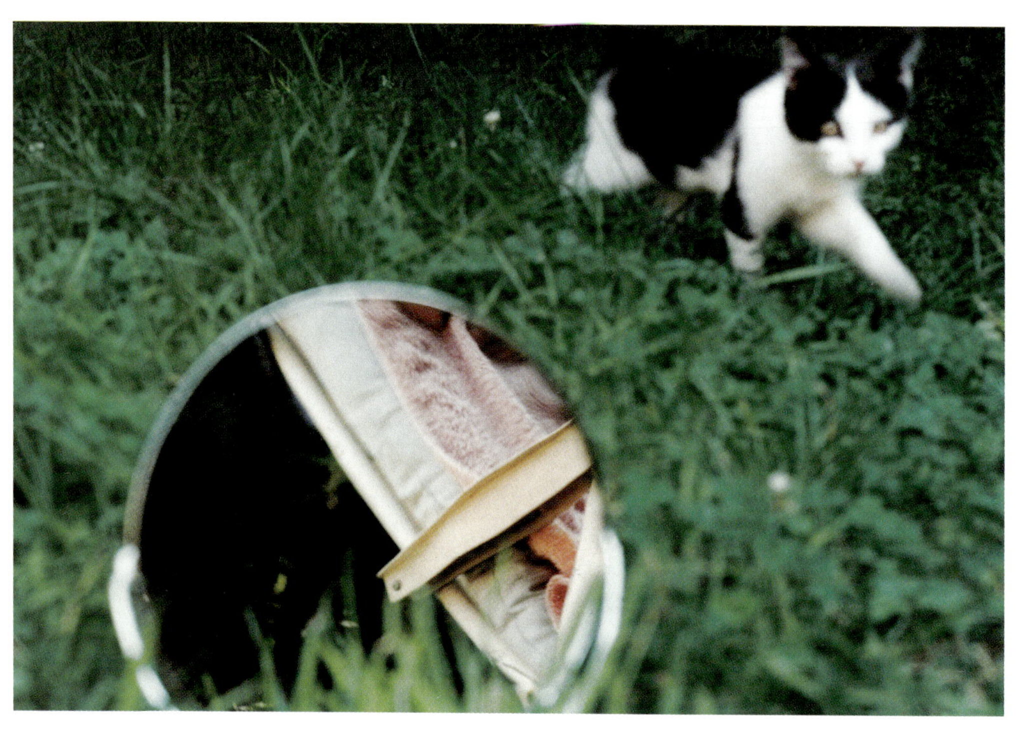

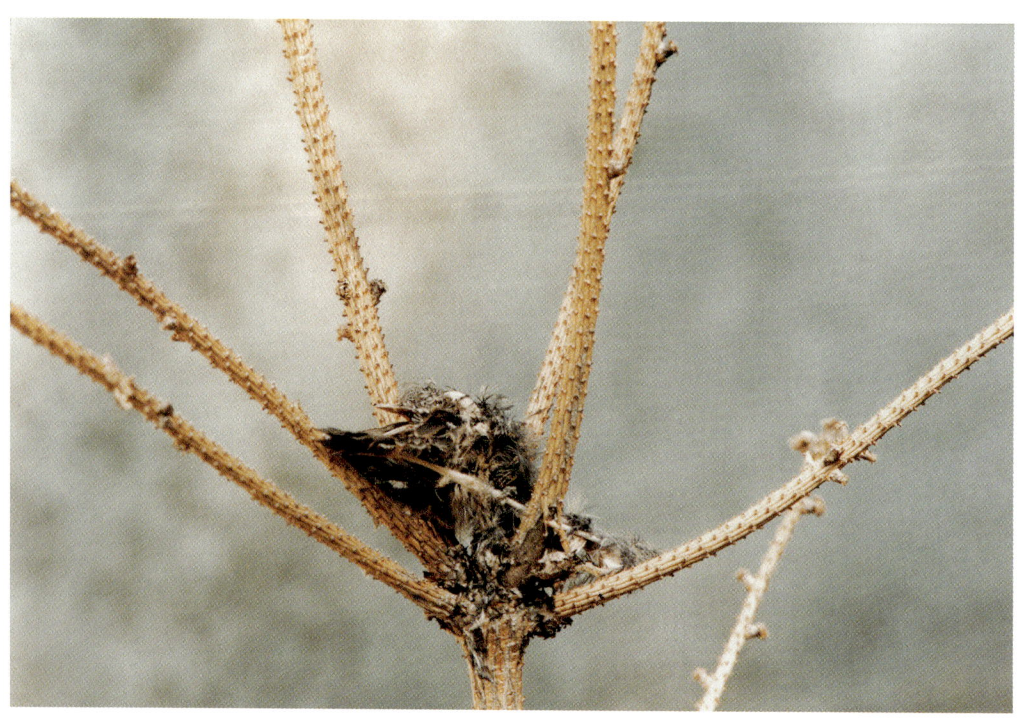

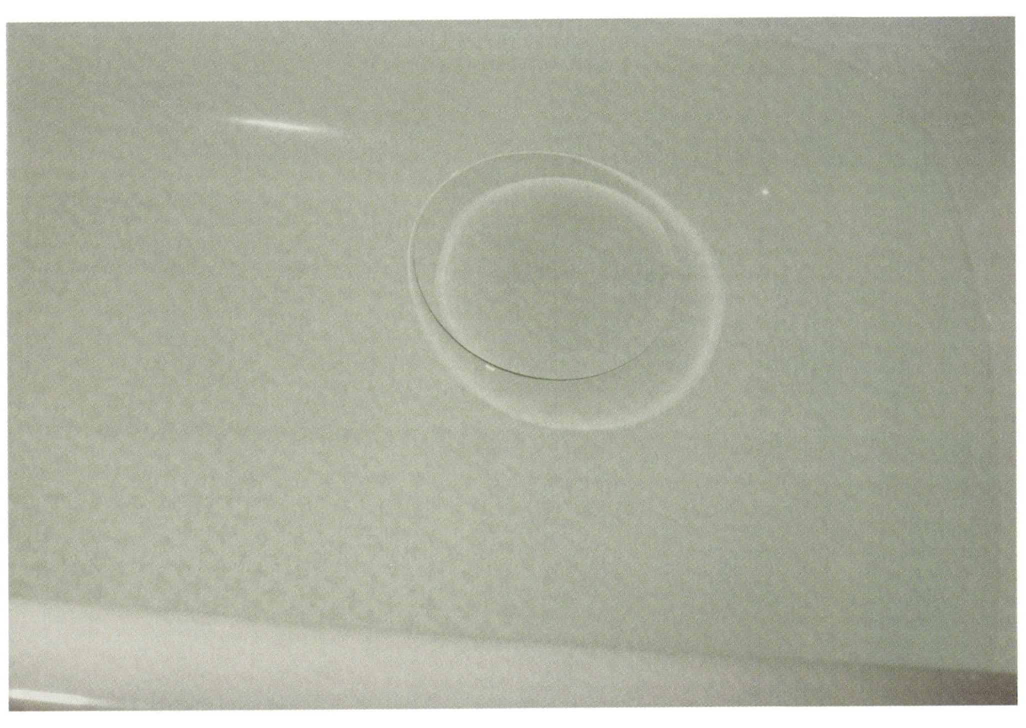

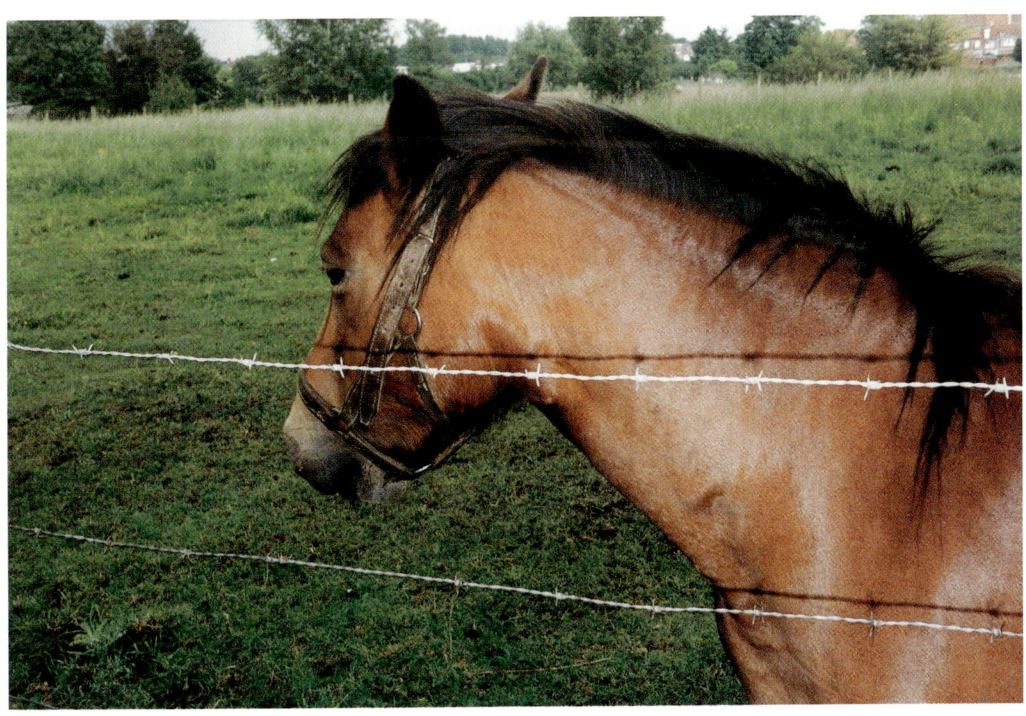

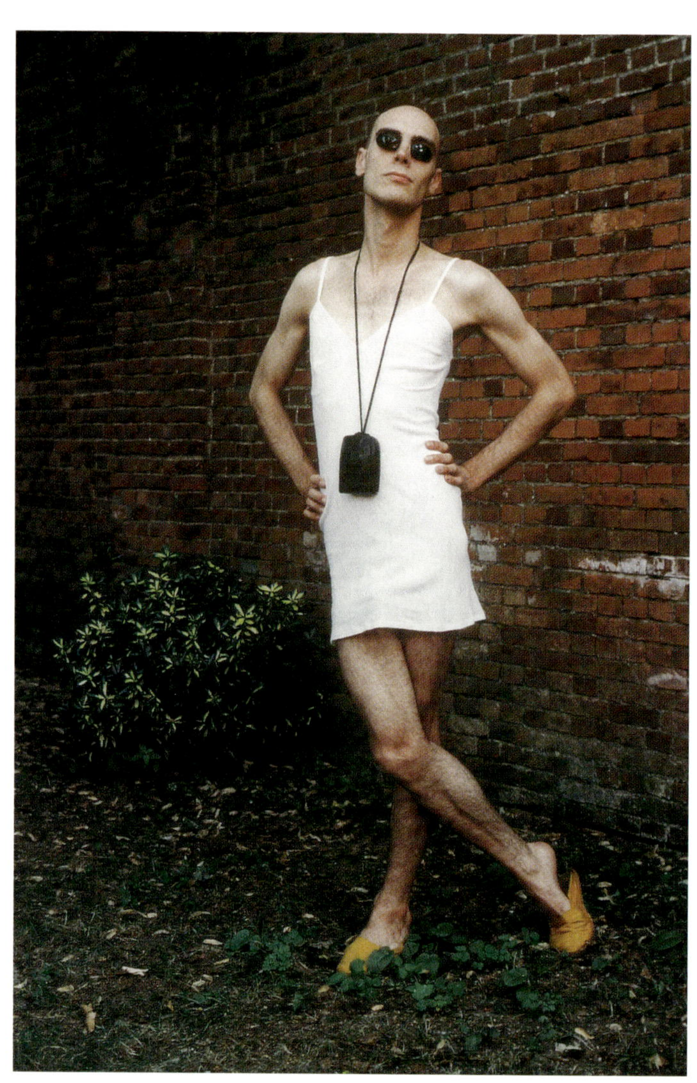

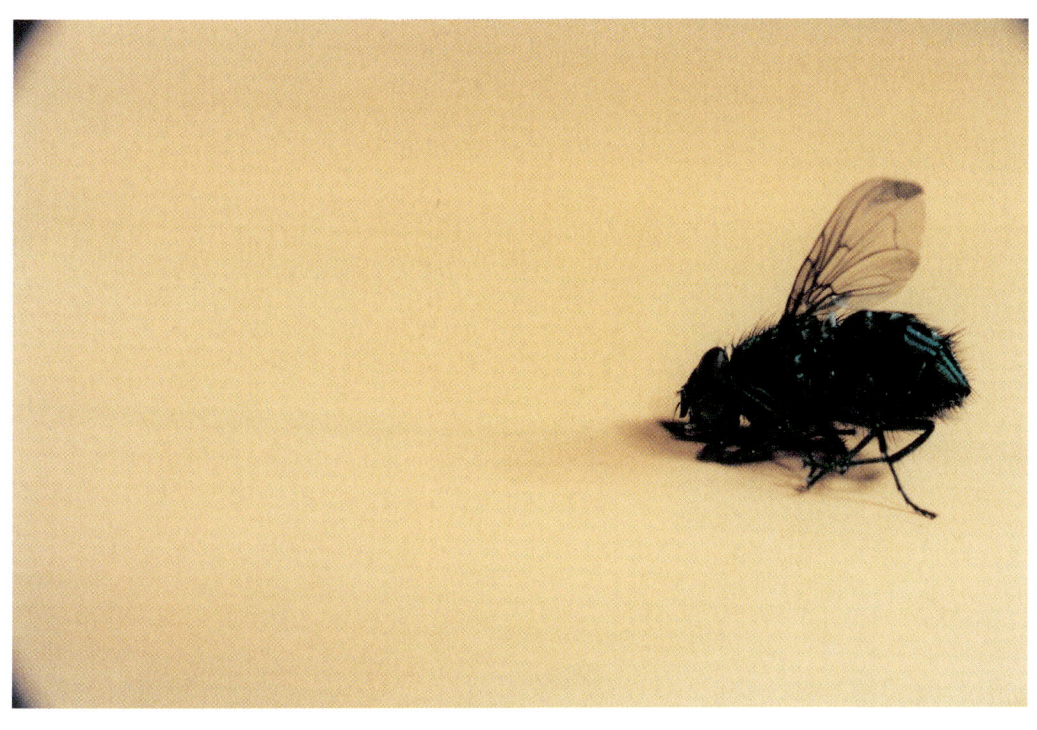

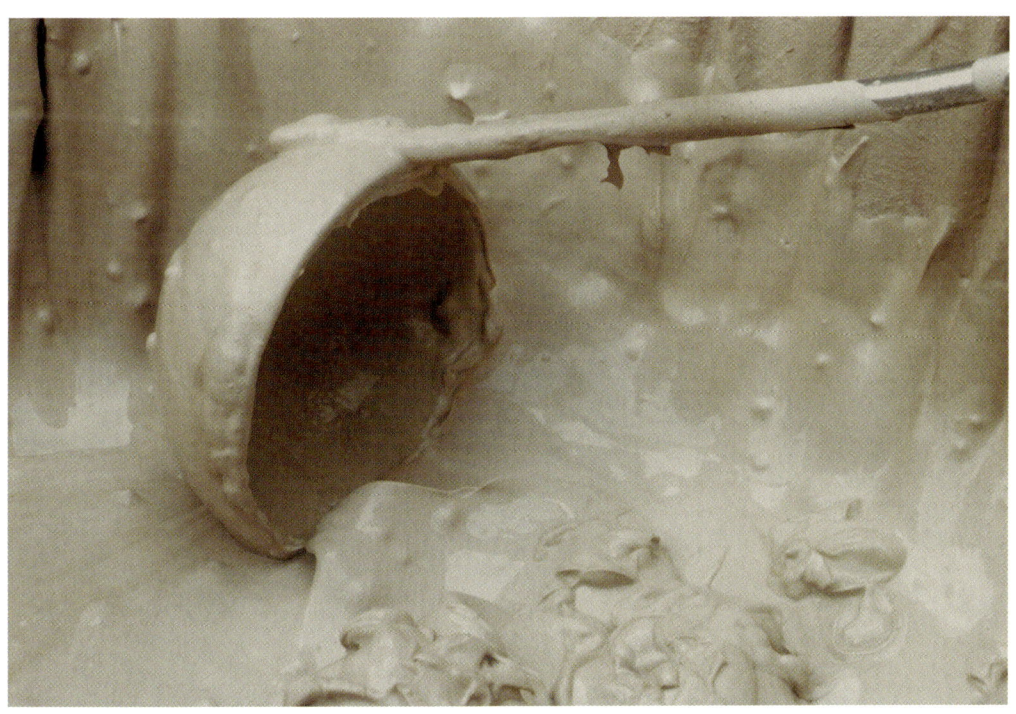

**

***

**
***

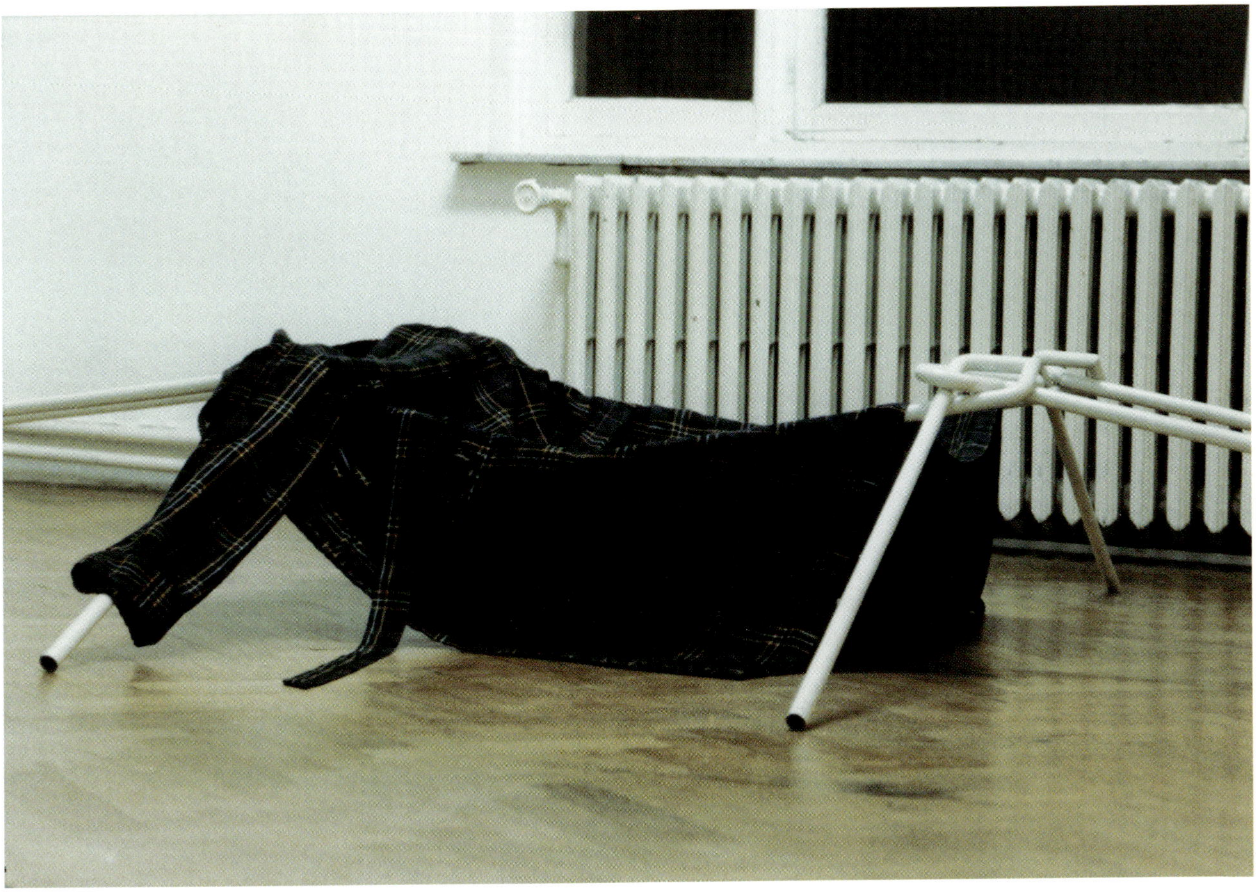

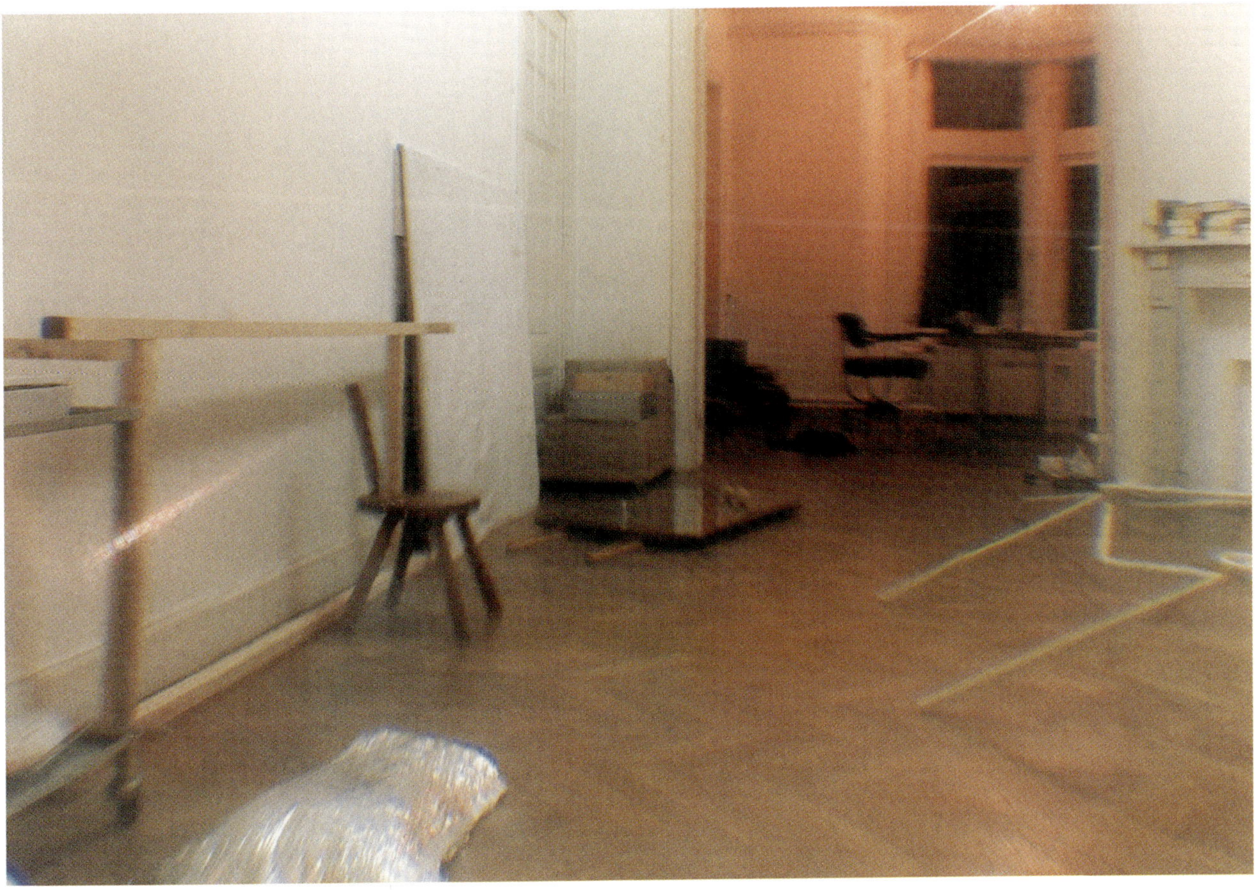

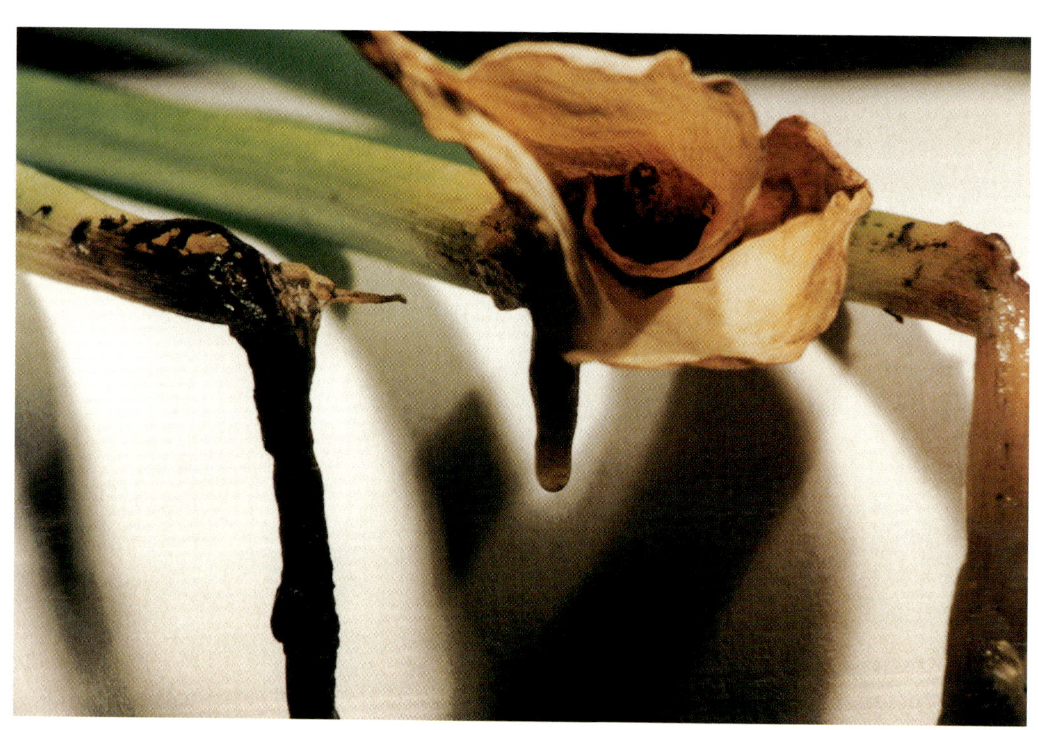

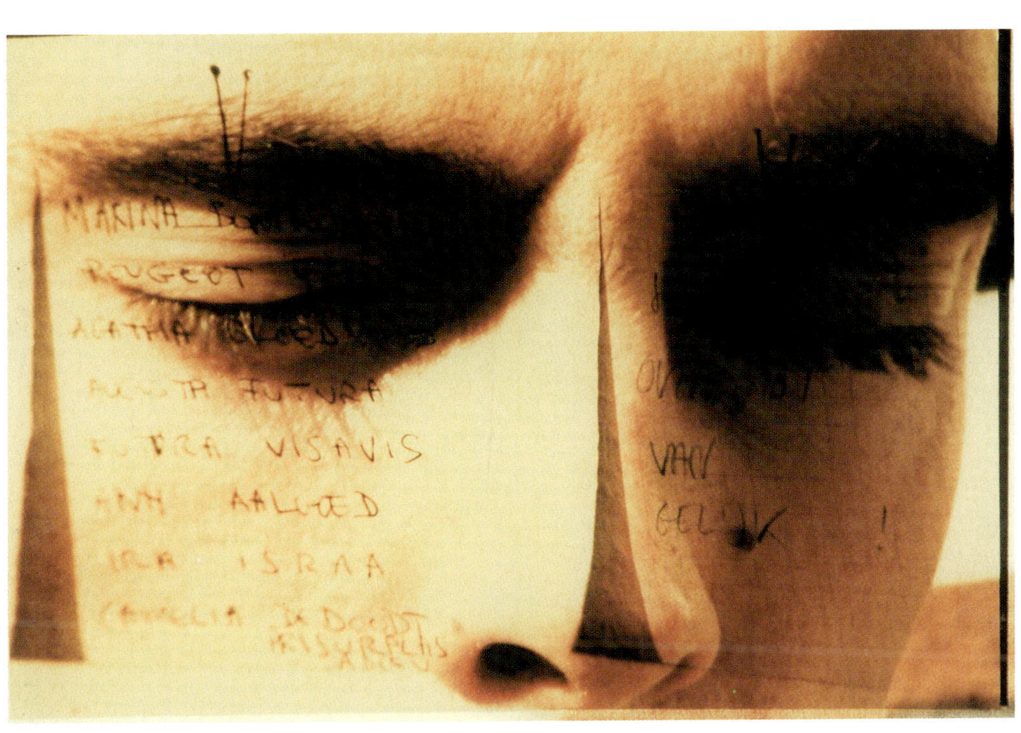

MARINA
PEUGEOT
AGATHA GLOED
FUTURA
FUTRA VISAVIS
ANN AALOED
ISRAA
VAN
GELUK !

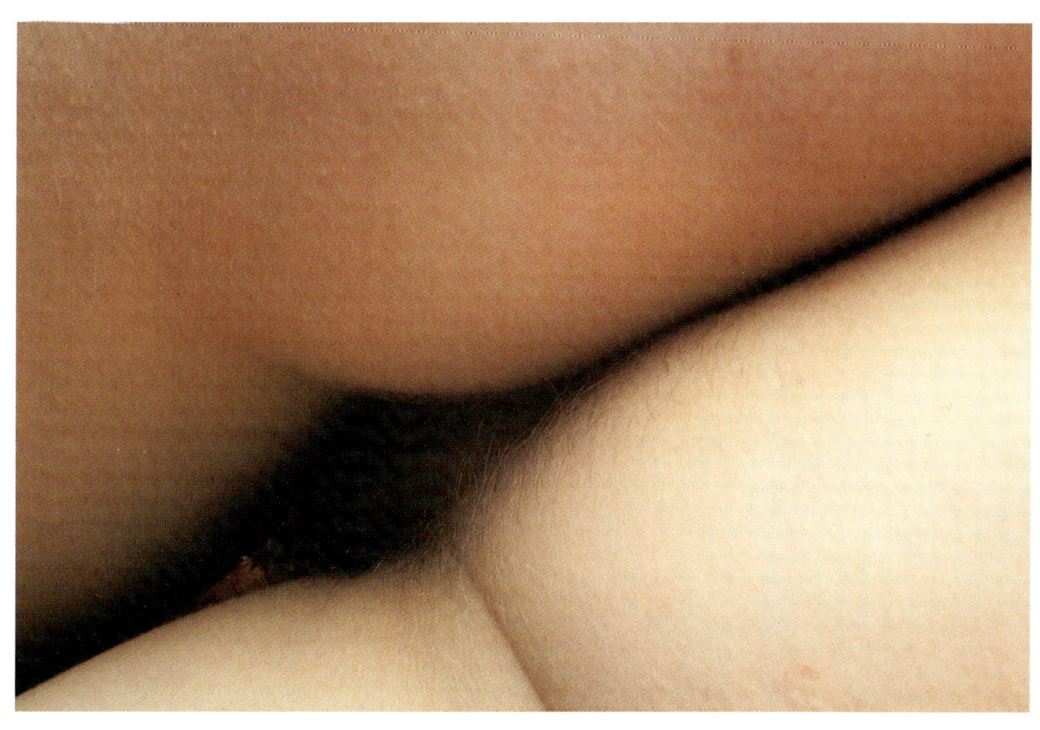

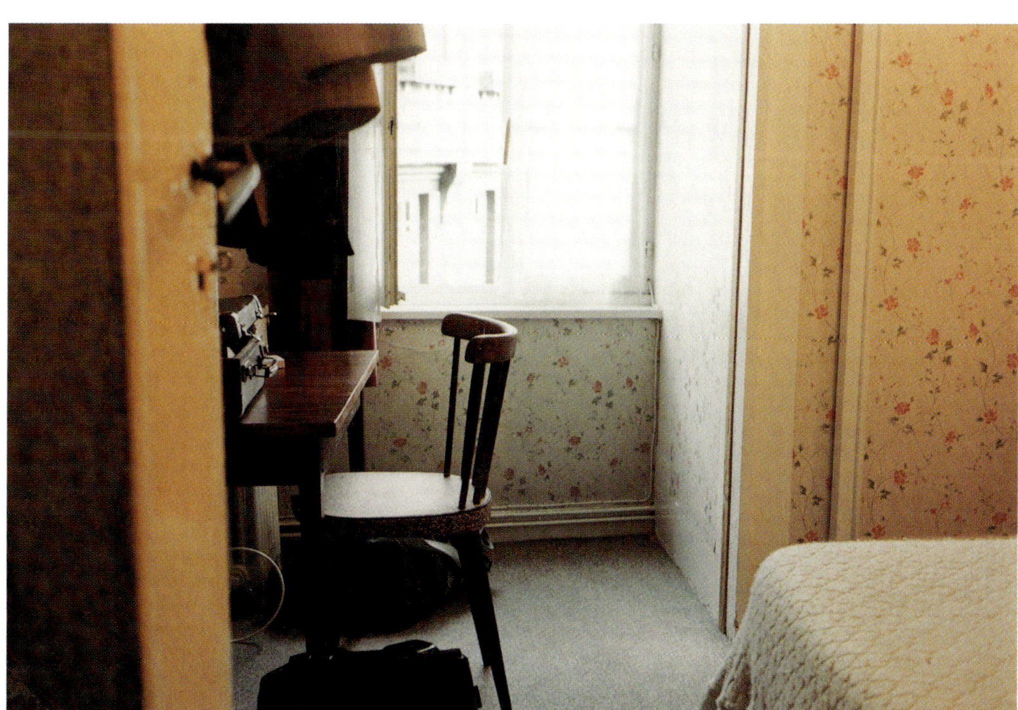

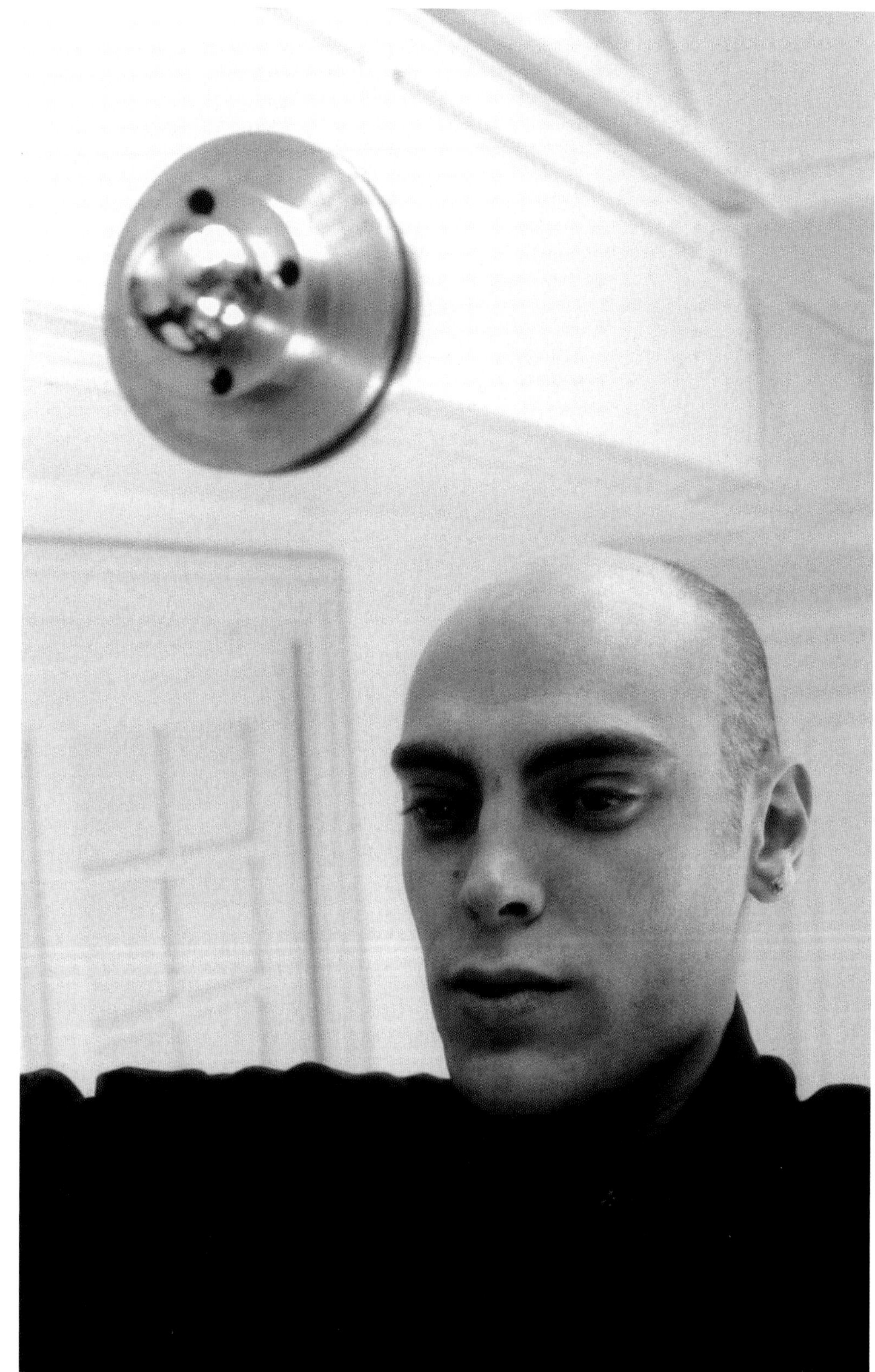

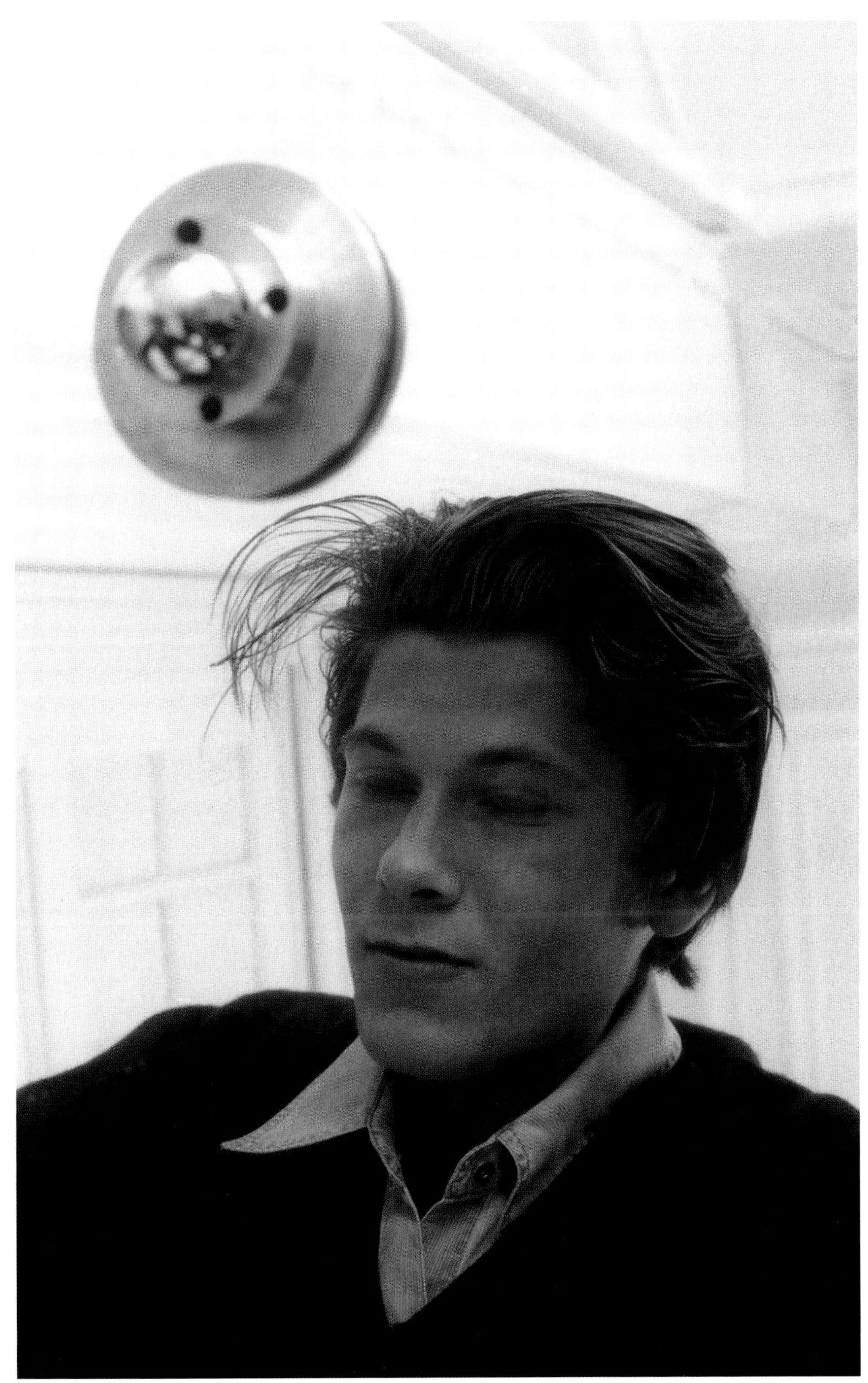

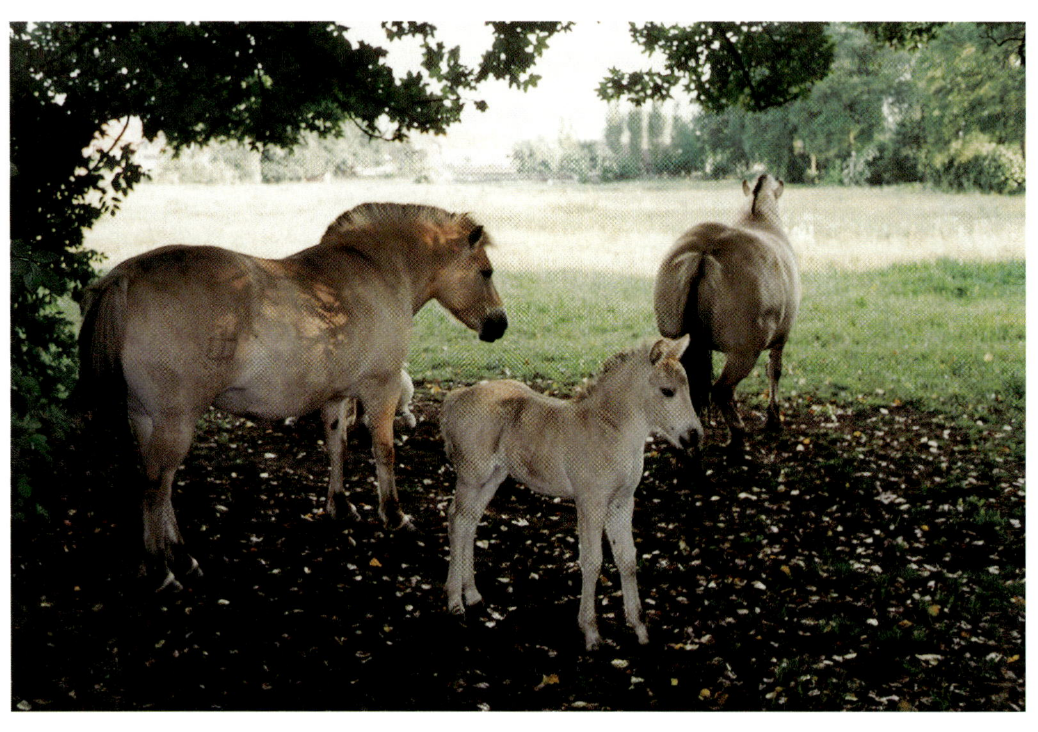

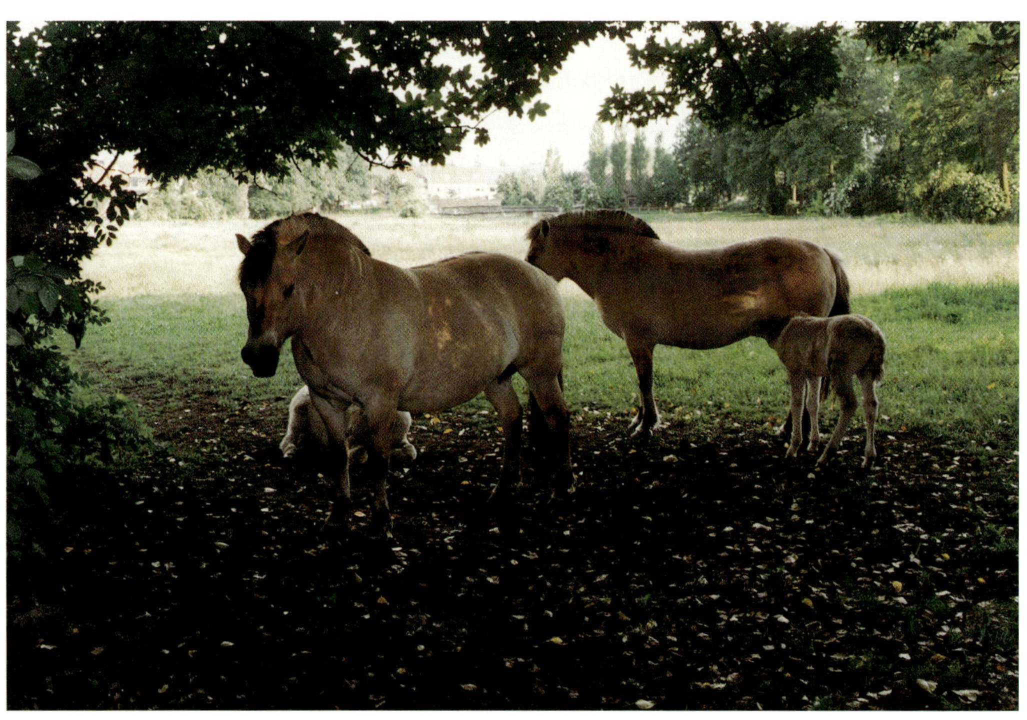

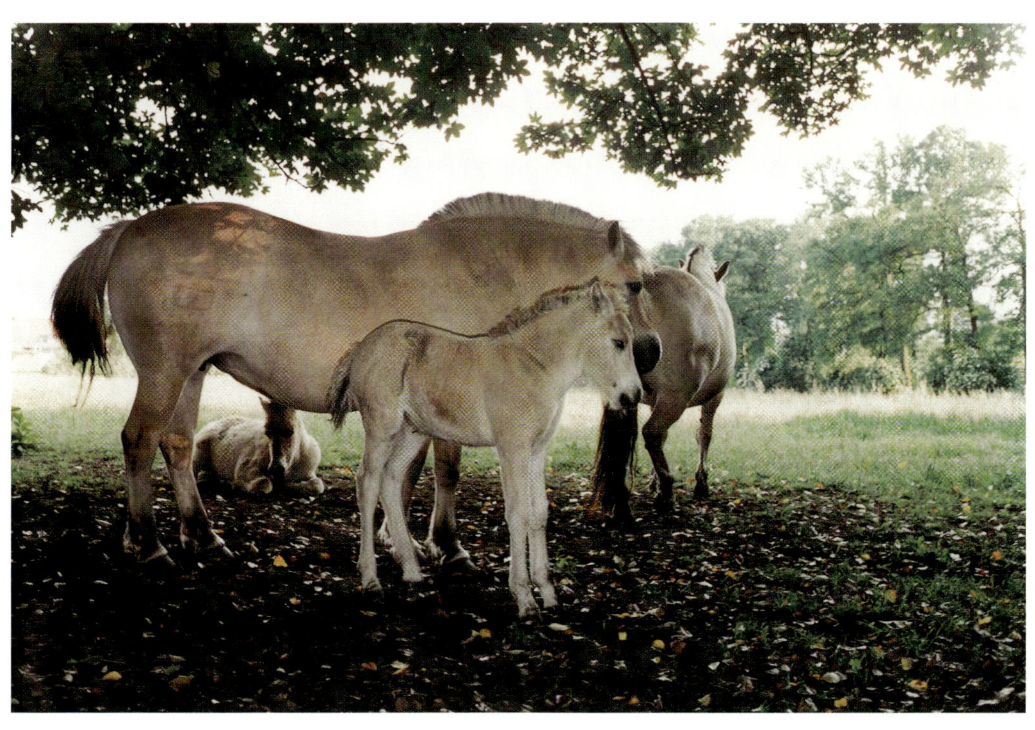

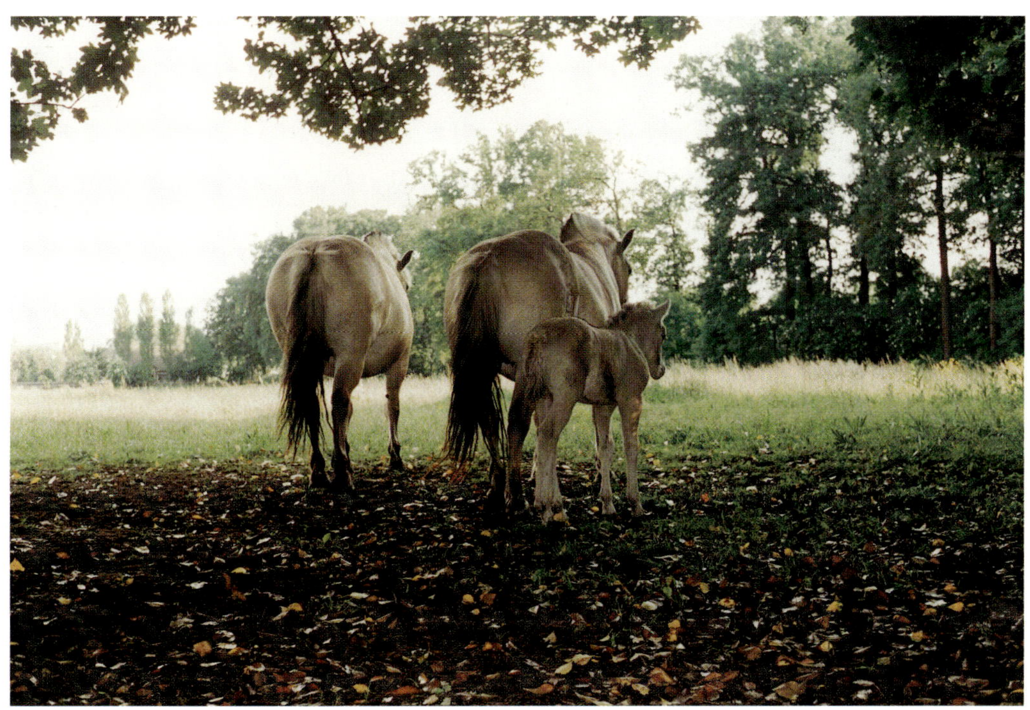

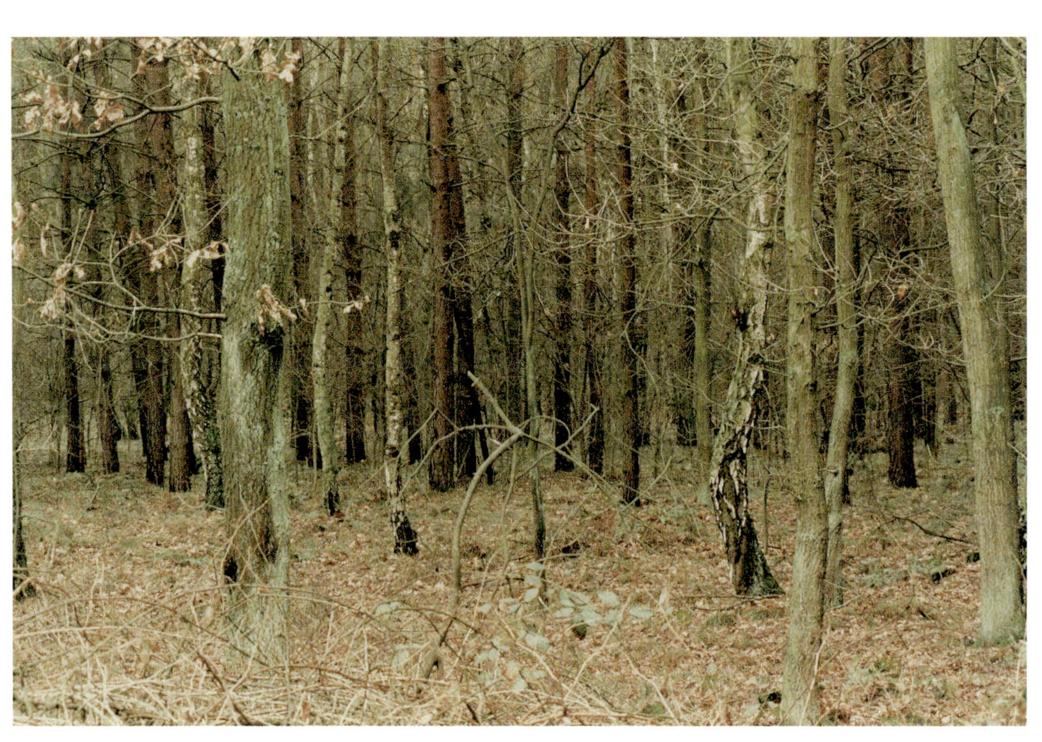

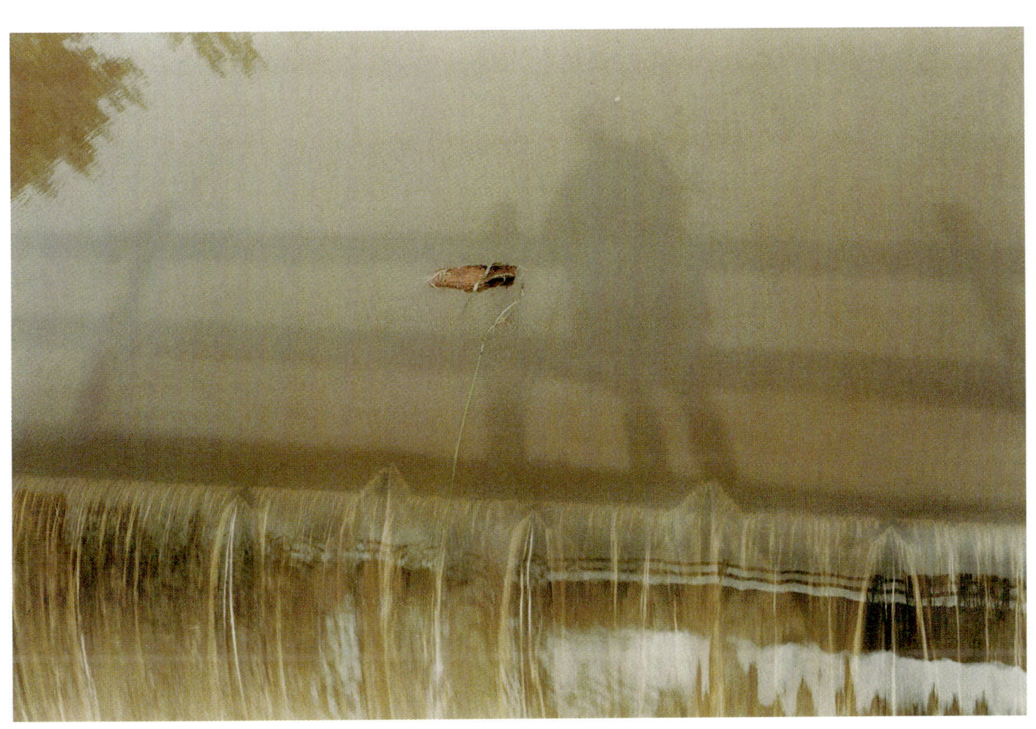

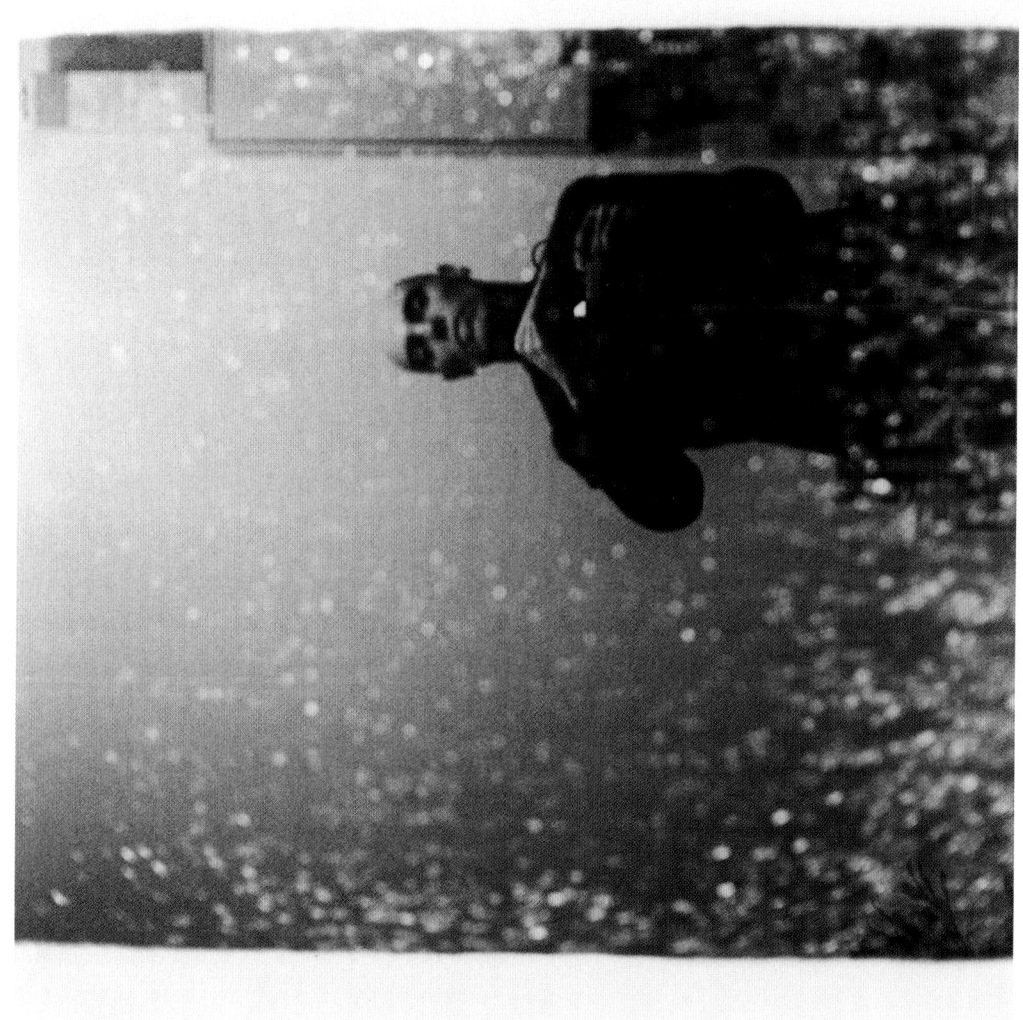

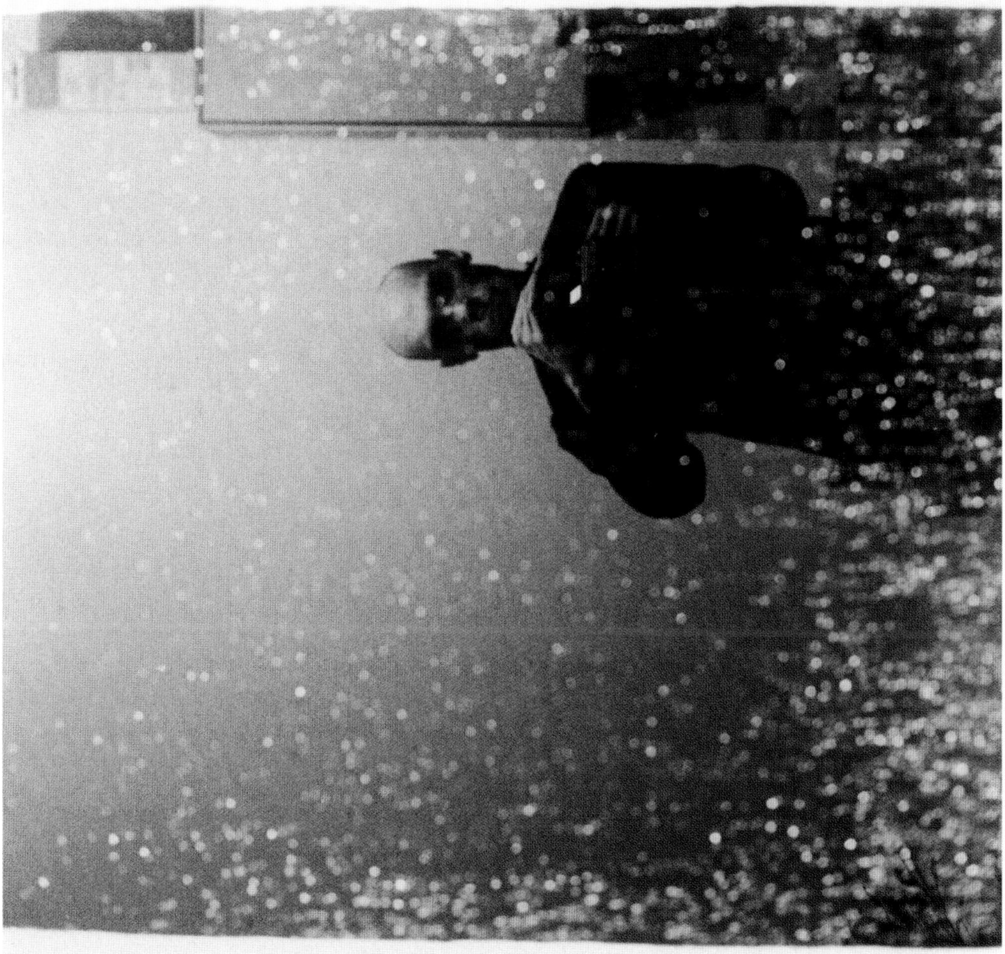

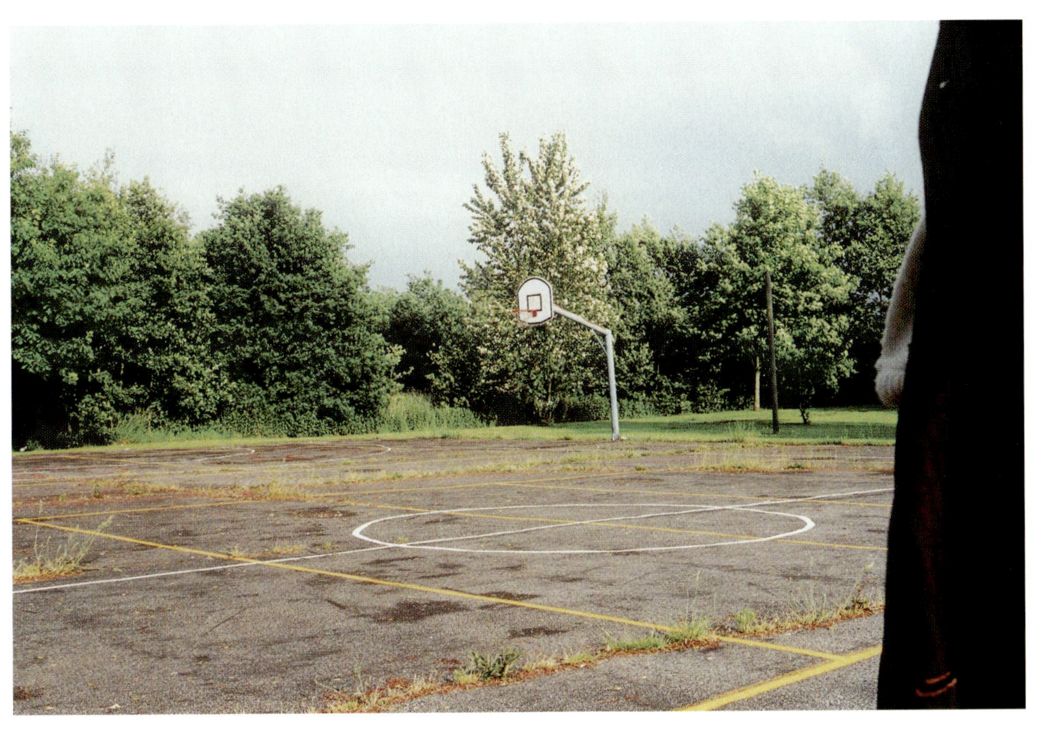

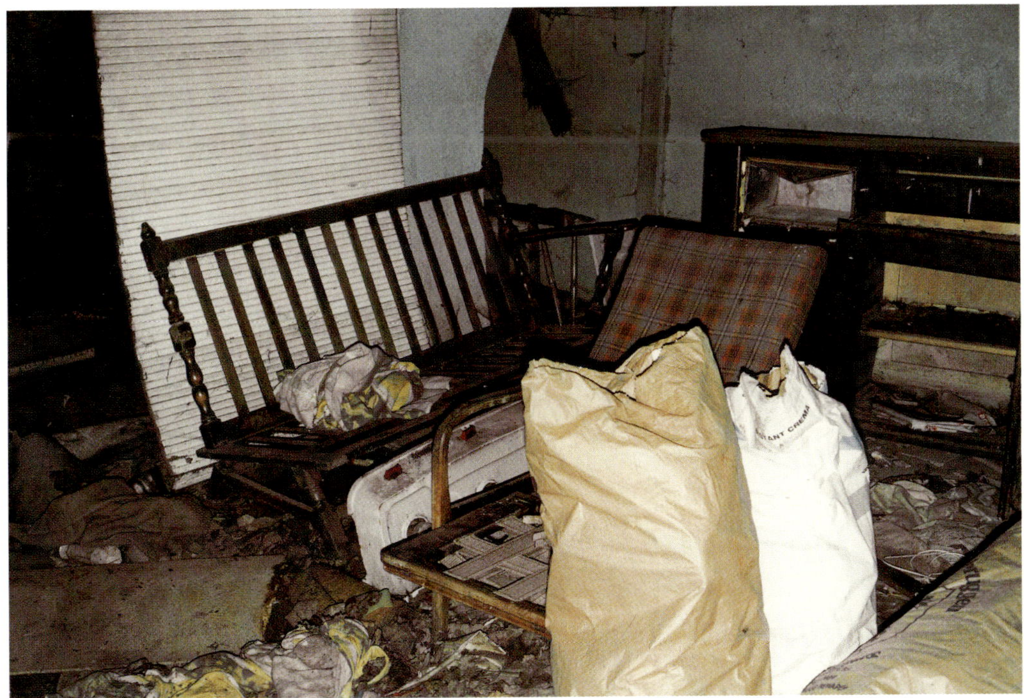

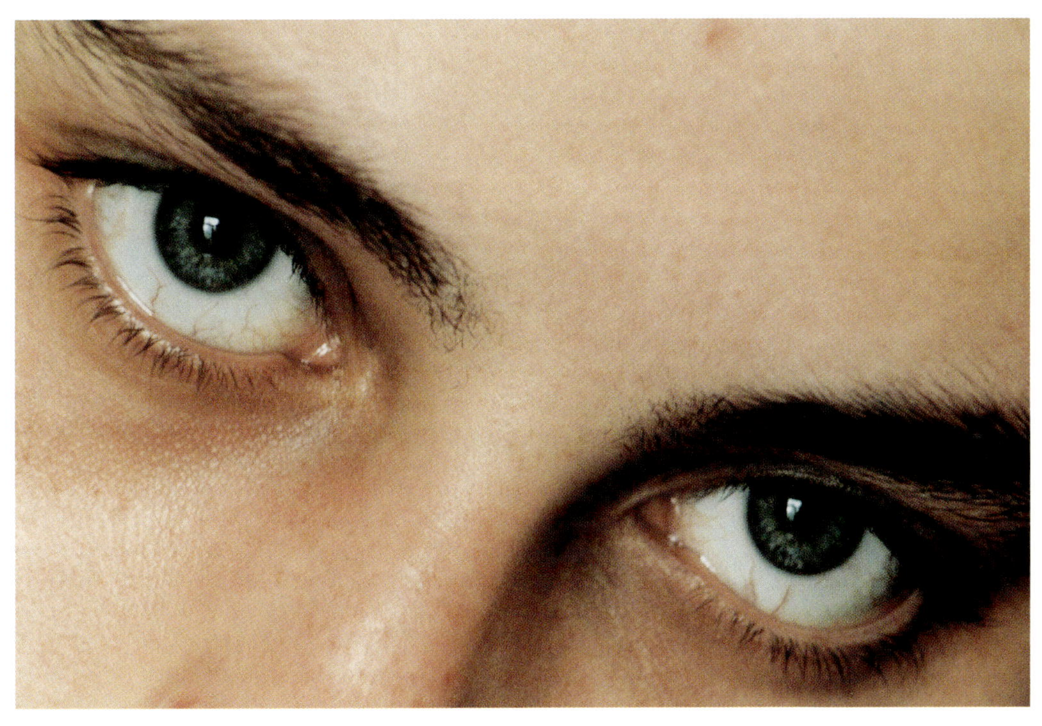

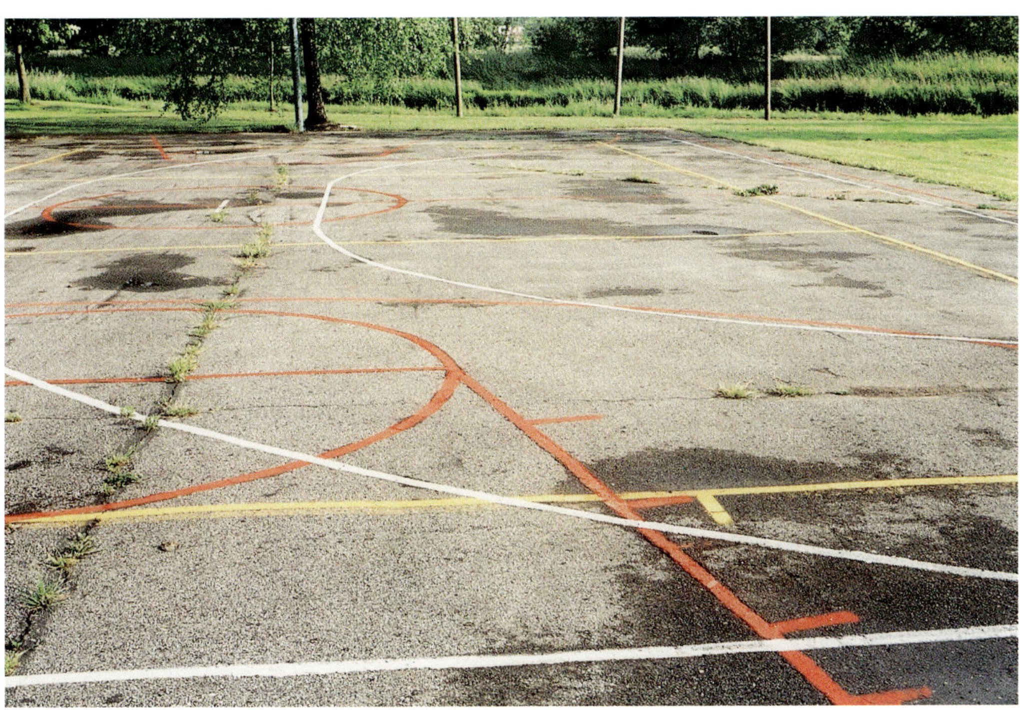

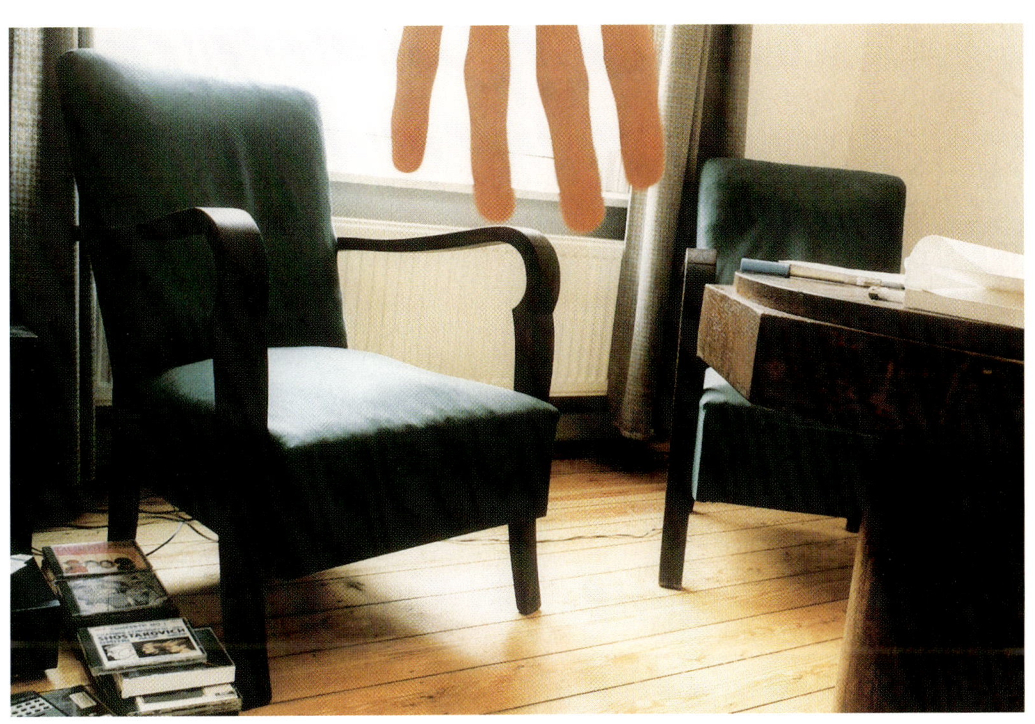

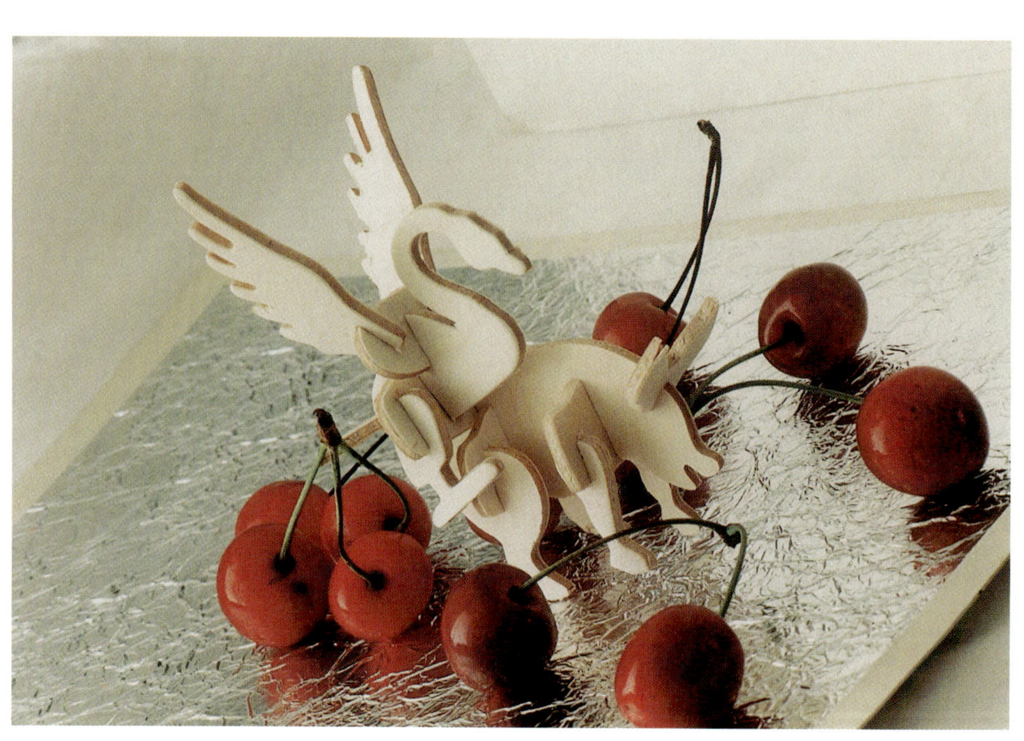

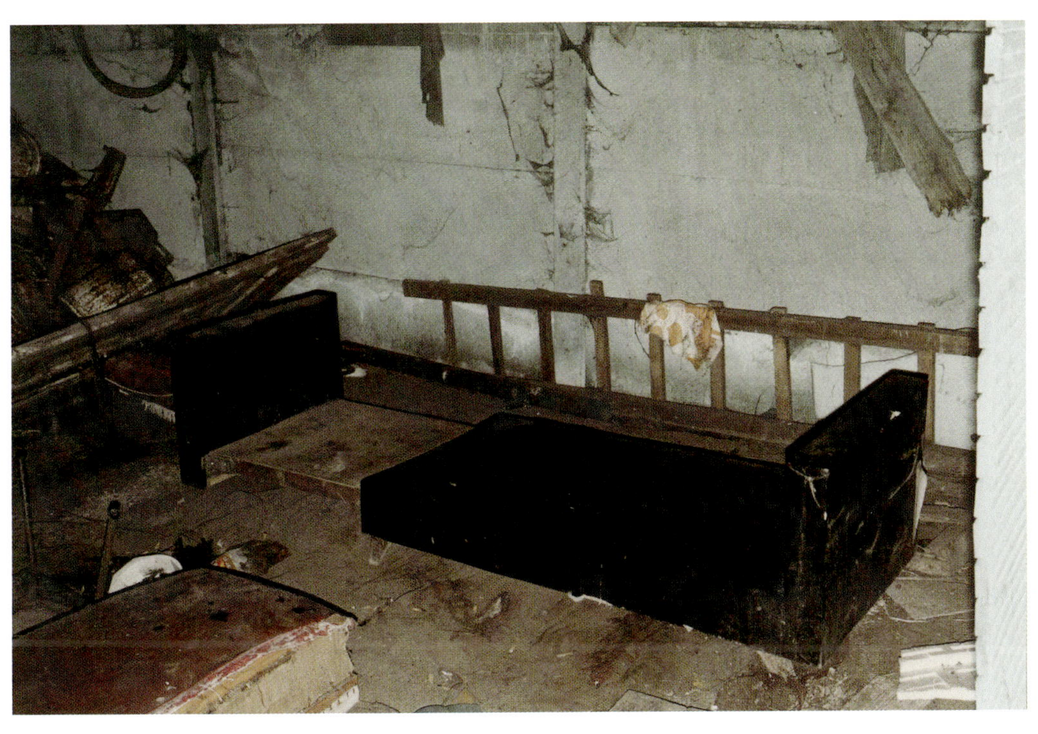

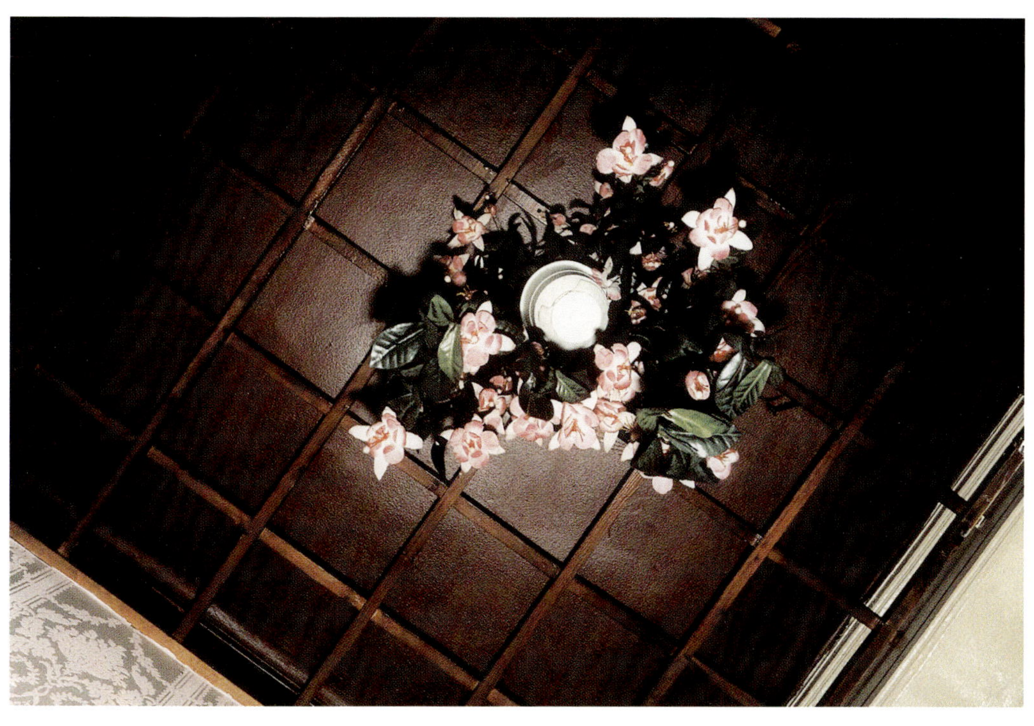

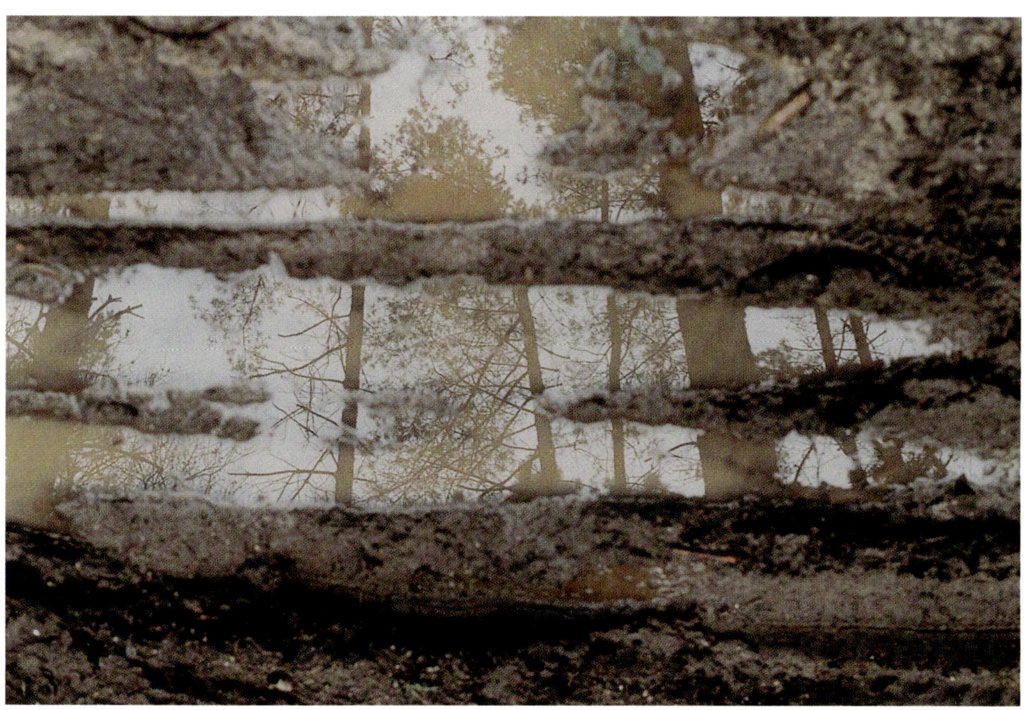

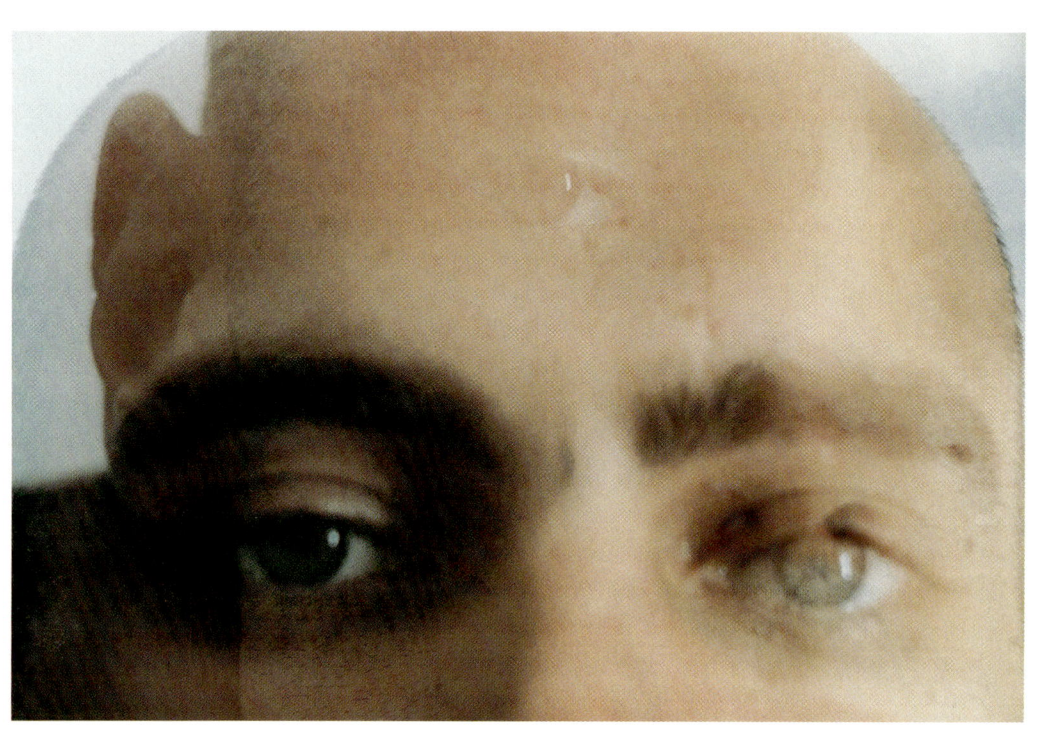

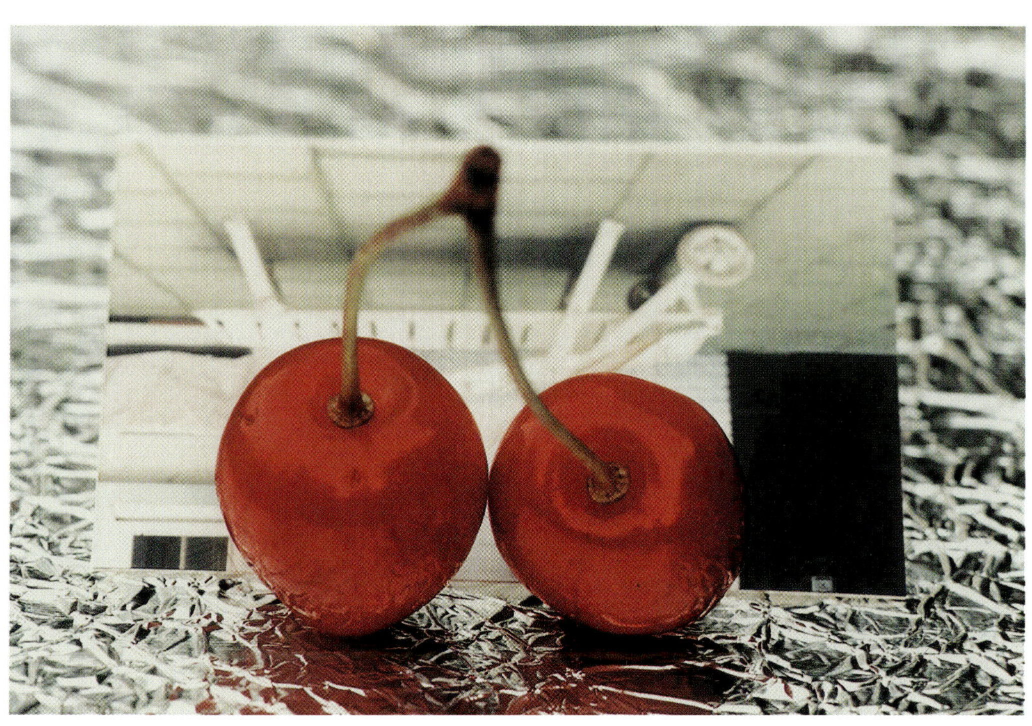

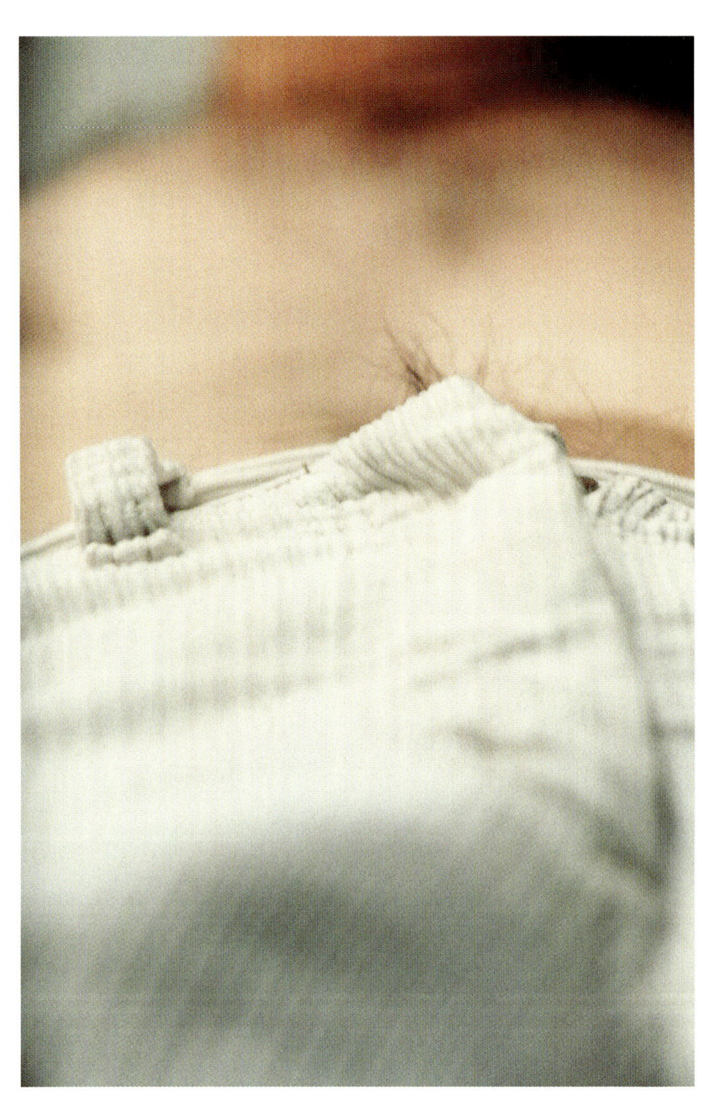

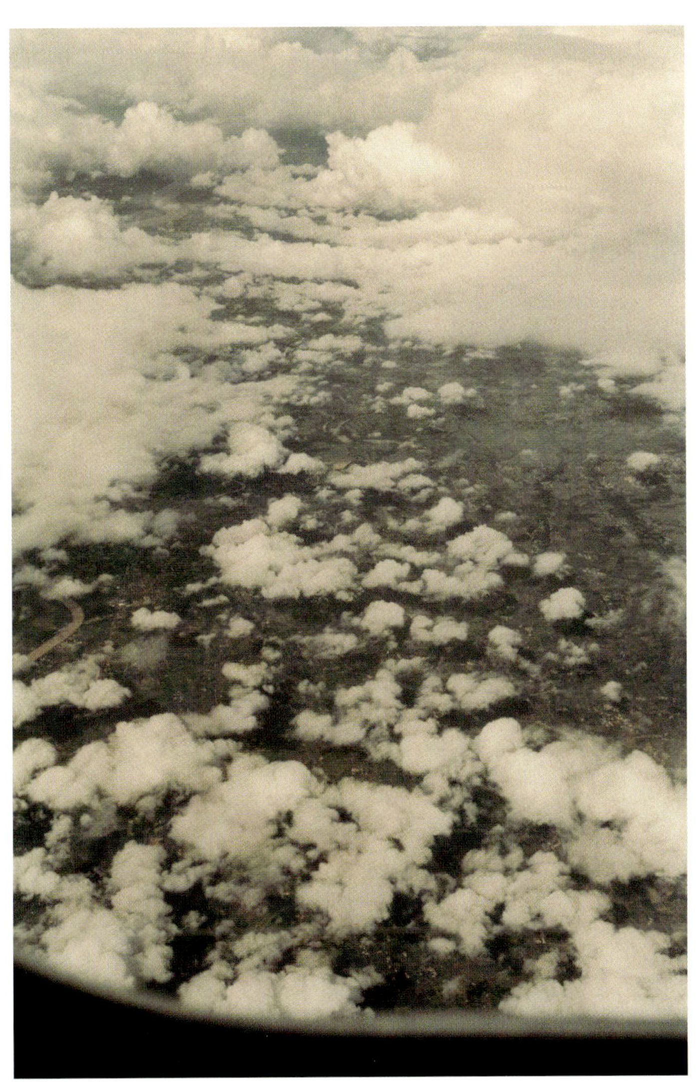

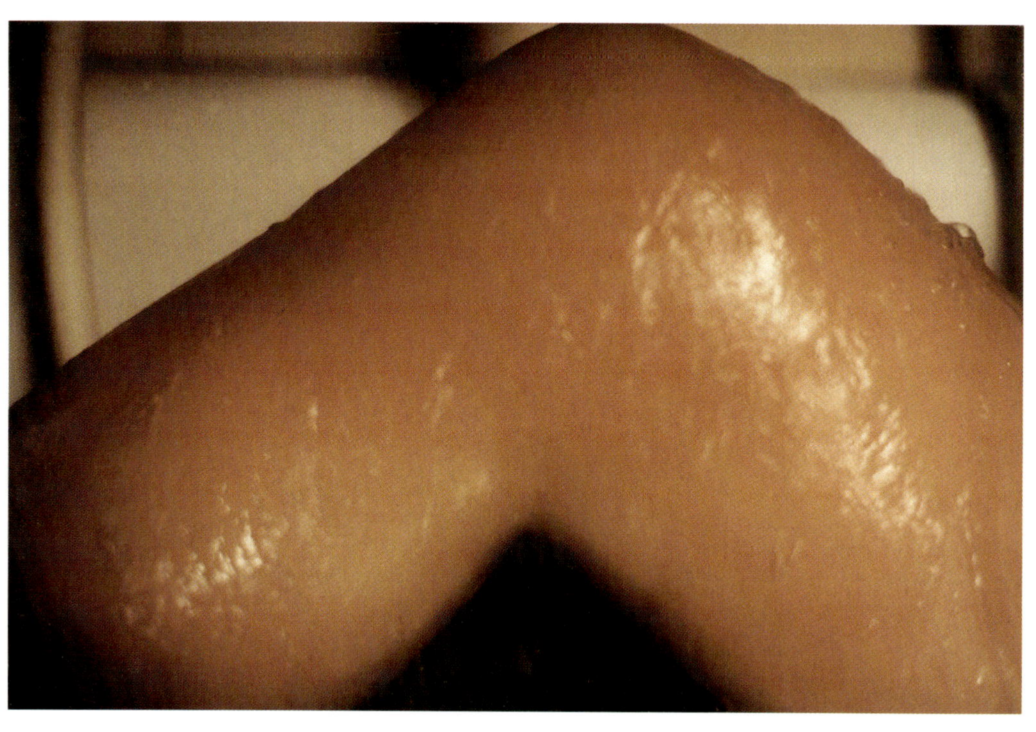

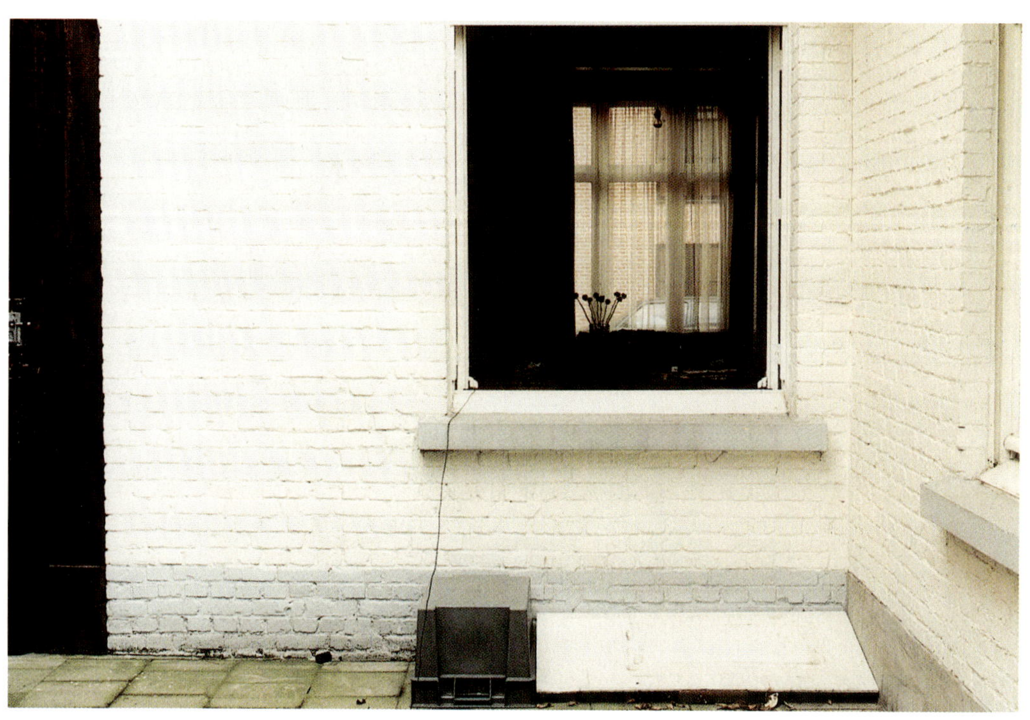

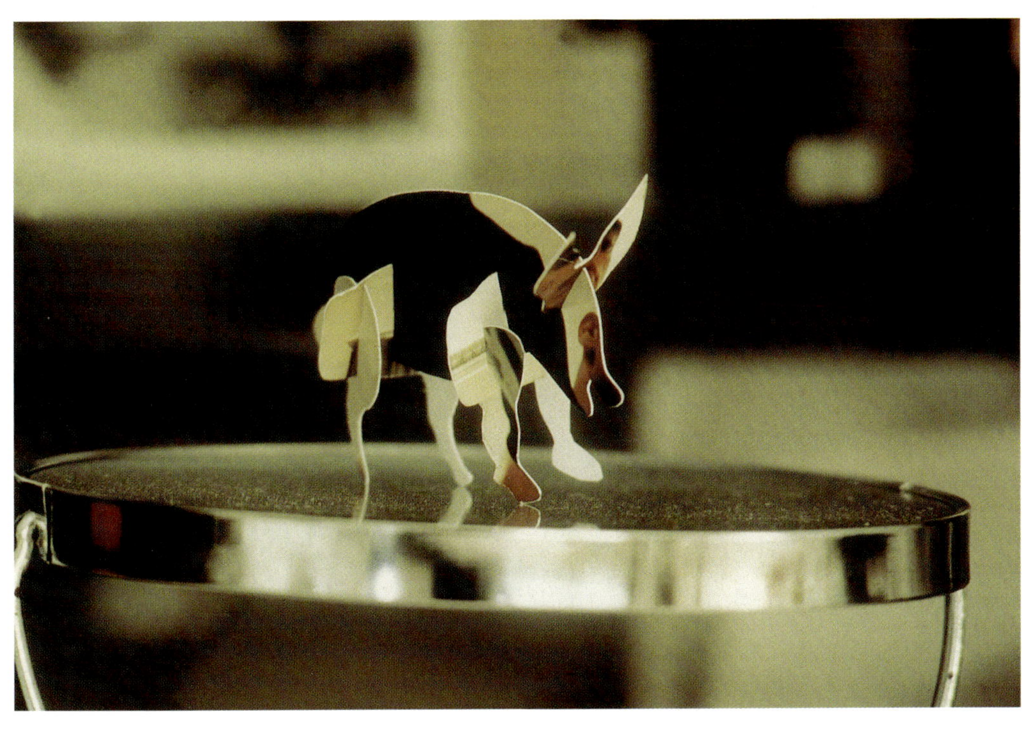

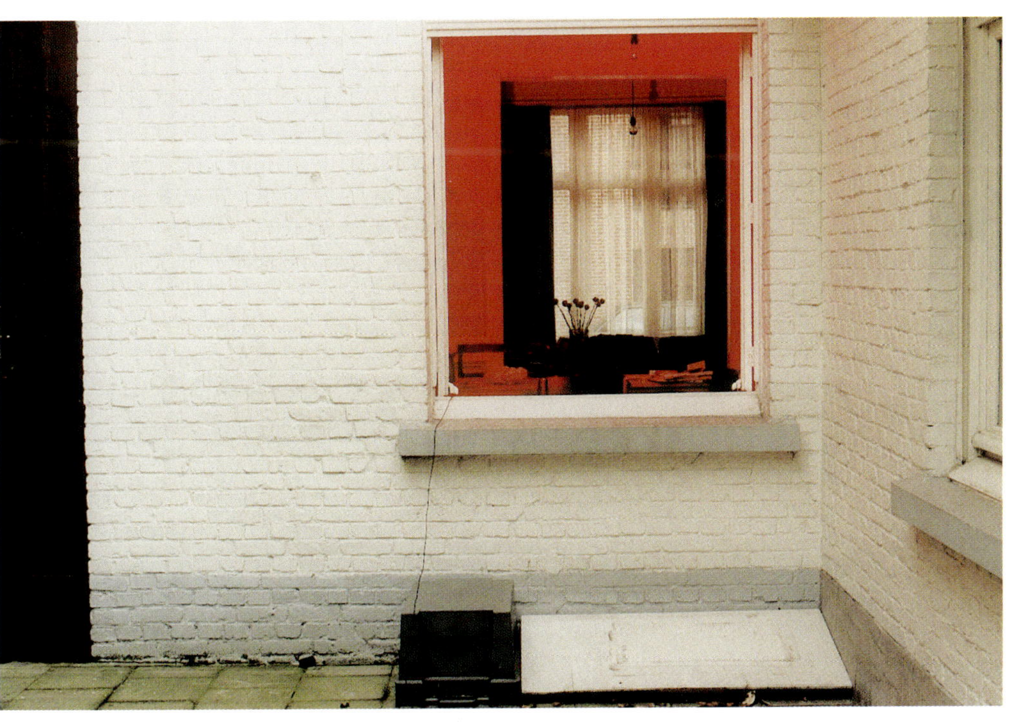

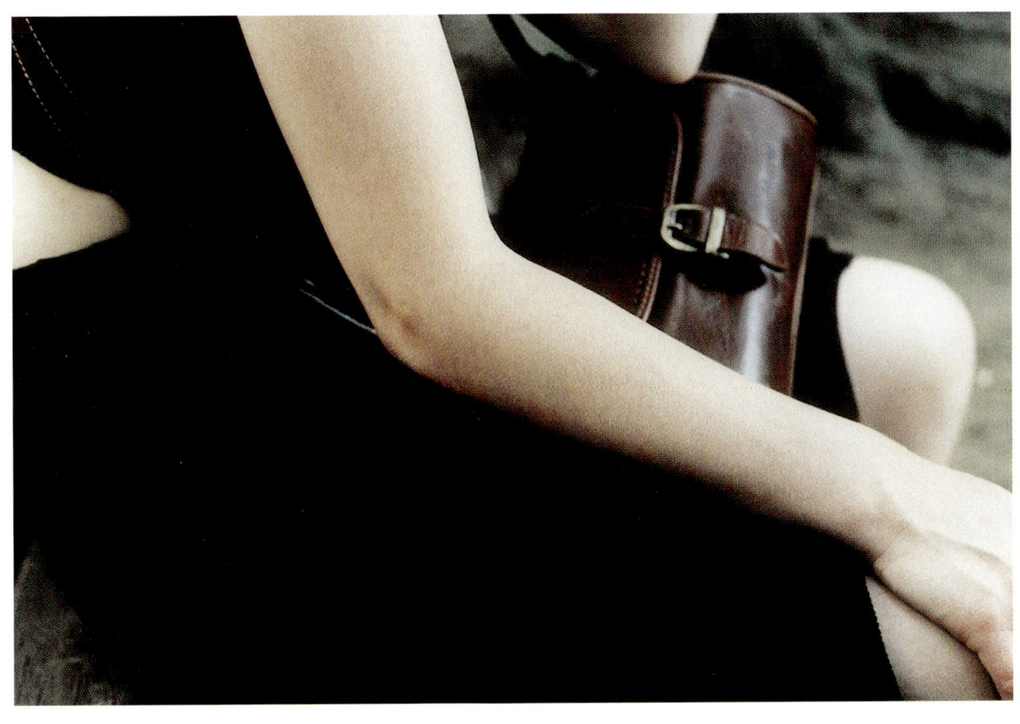

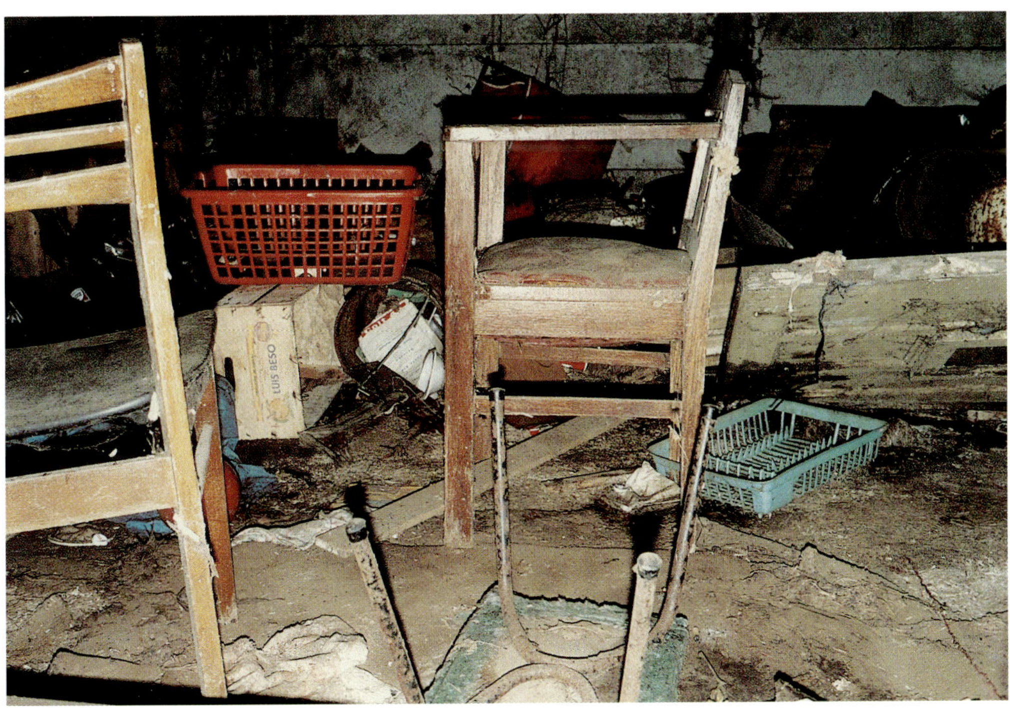

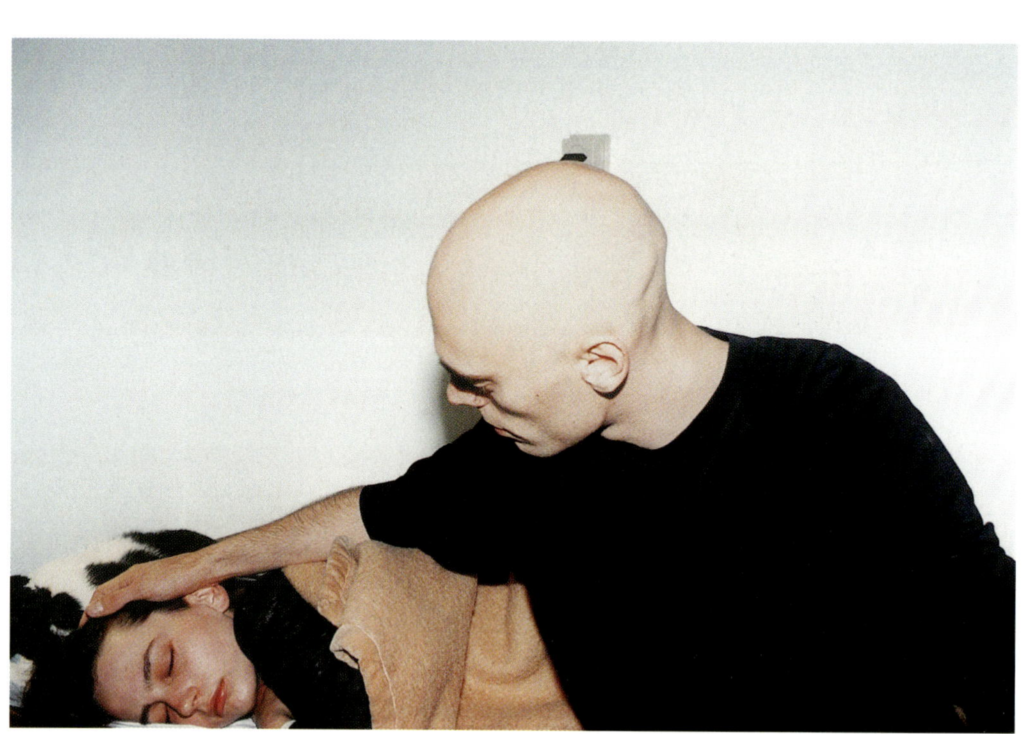

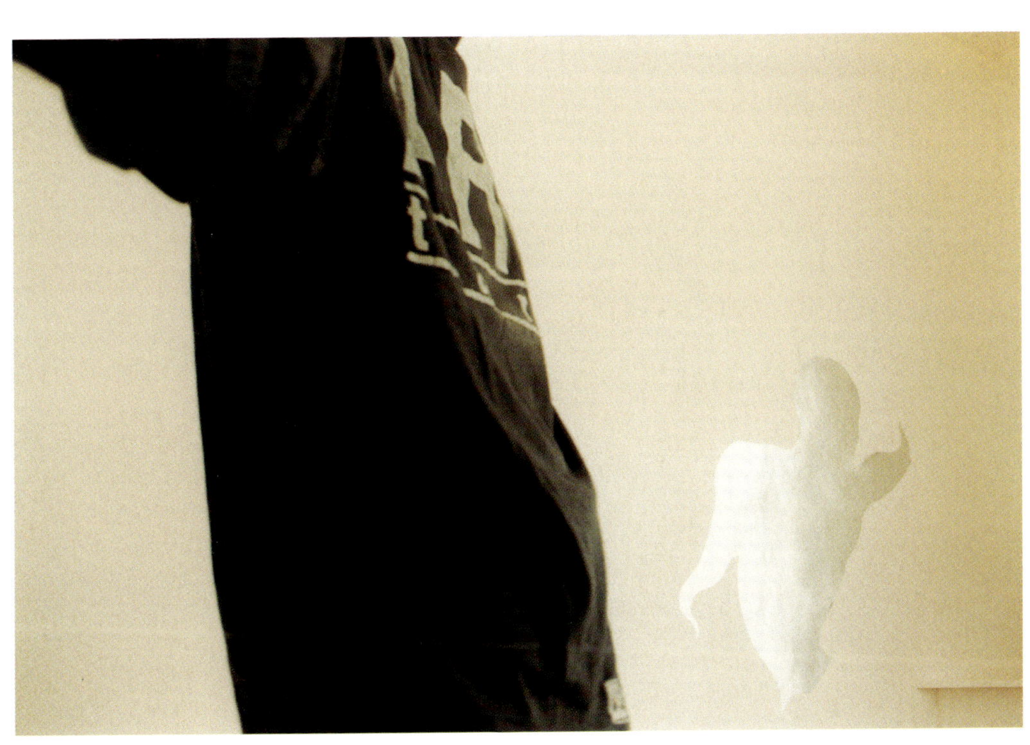

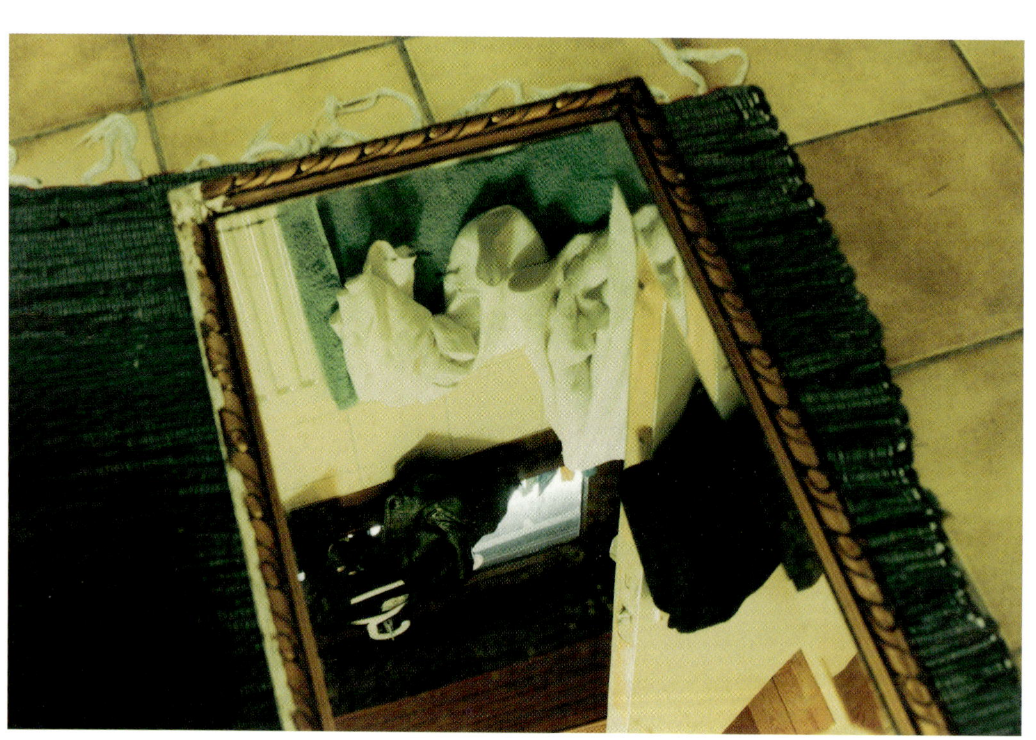

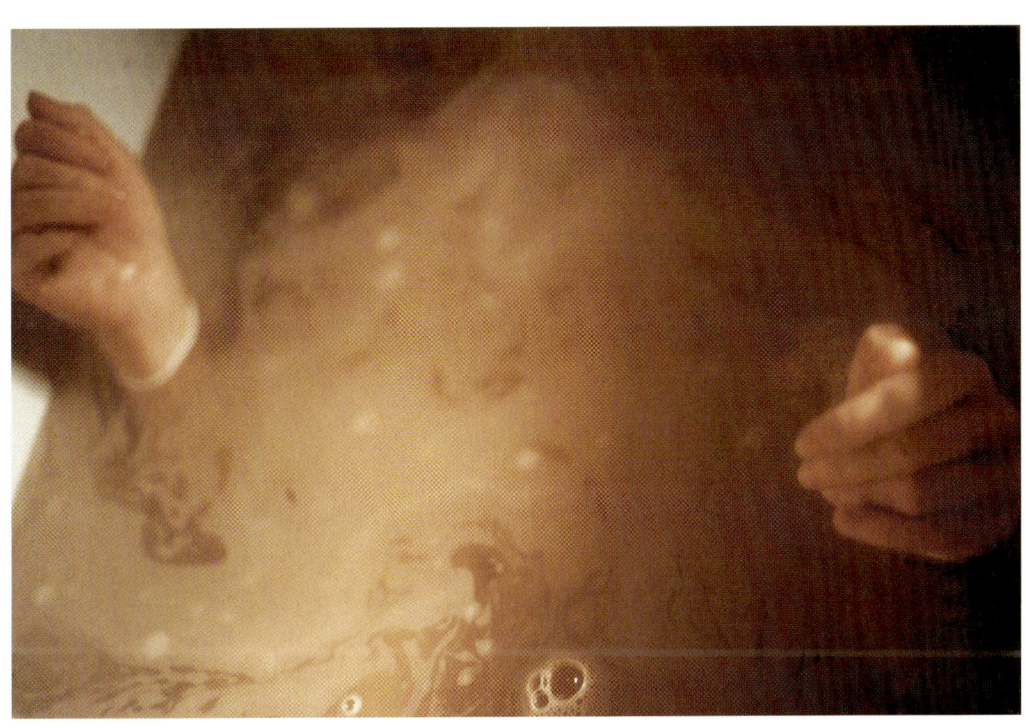

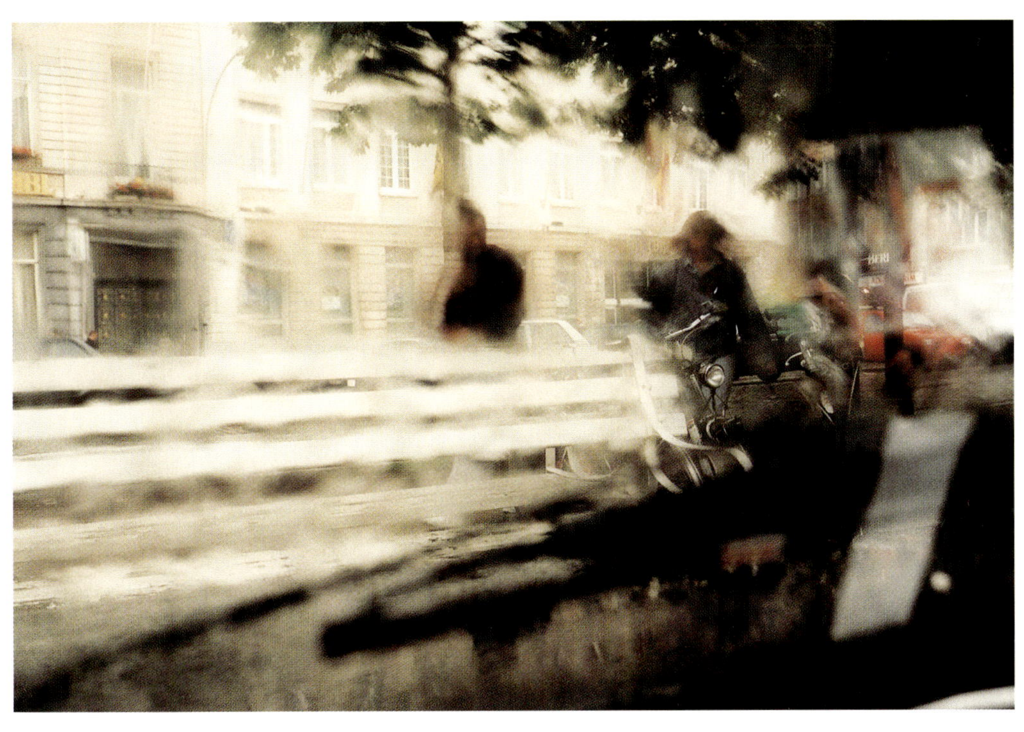

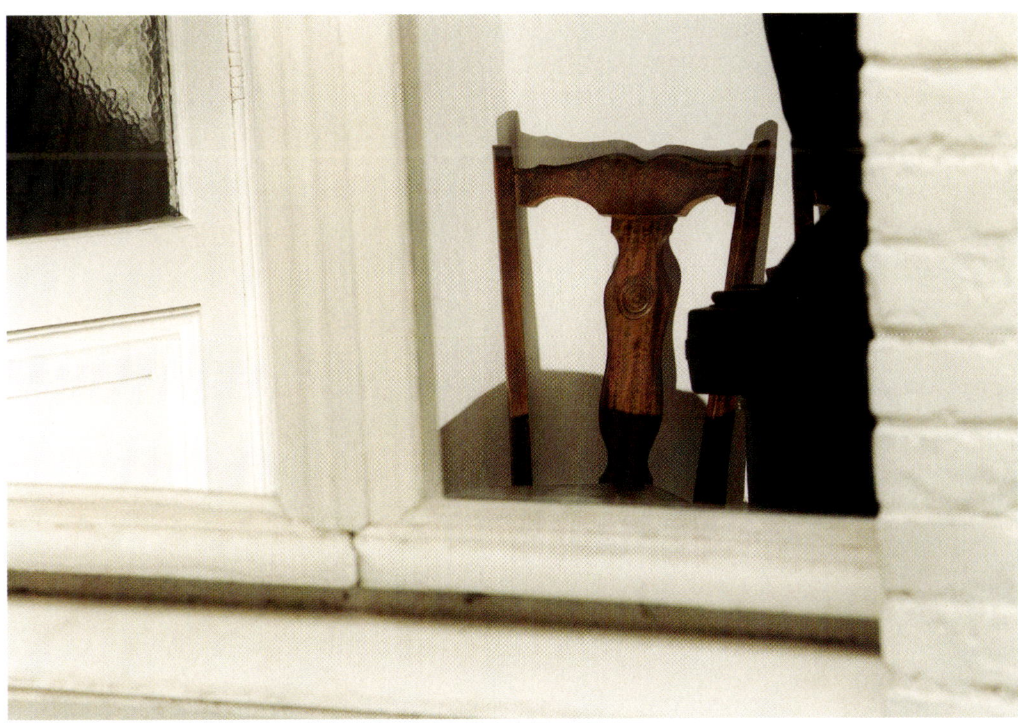

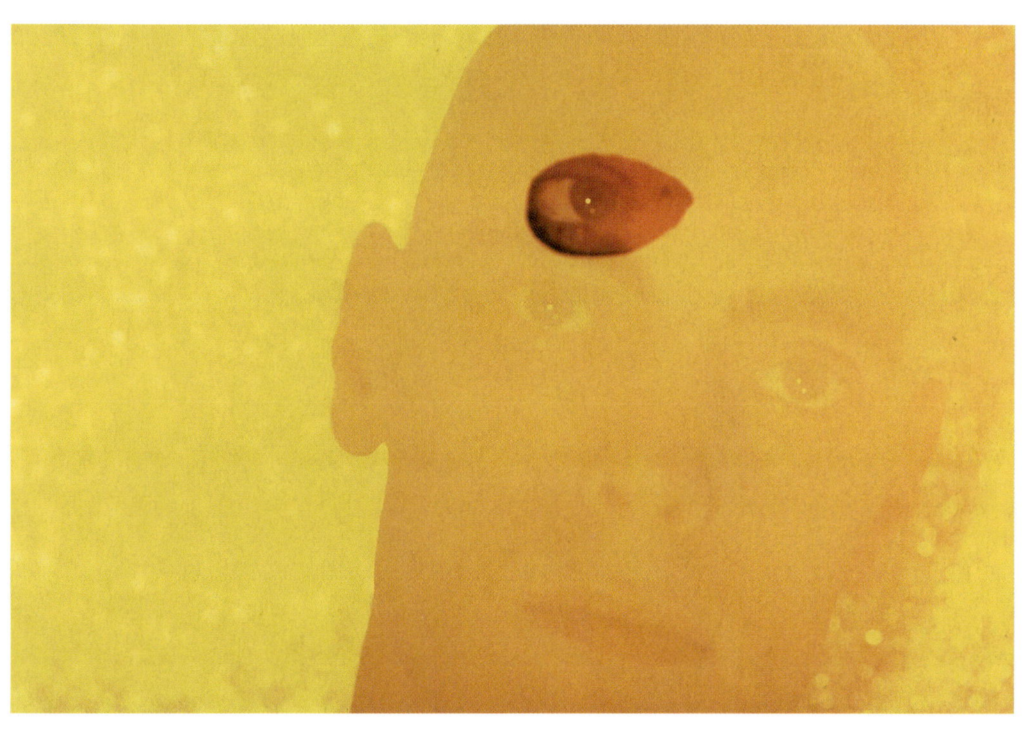

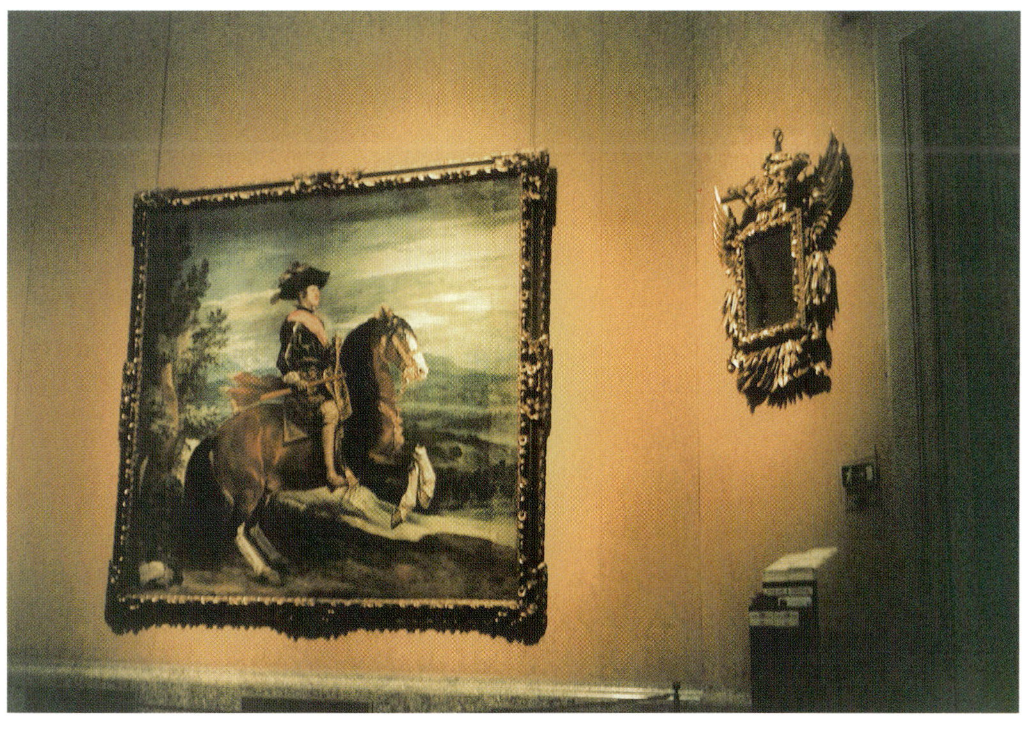

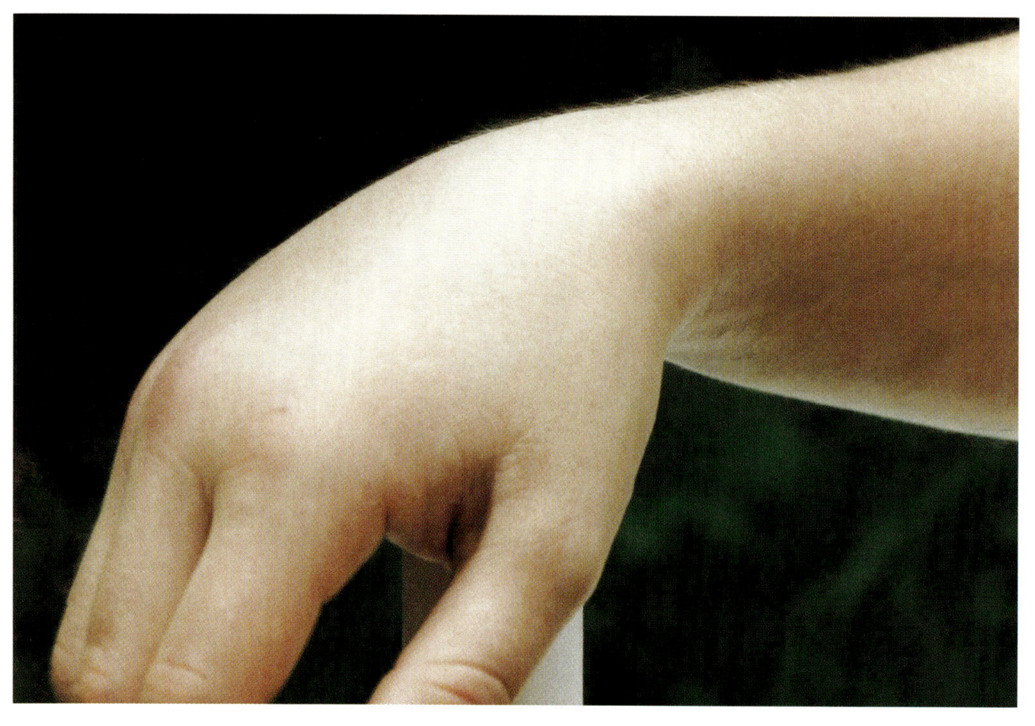

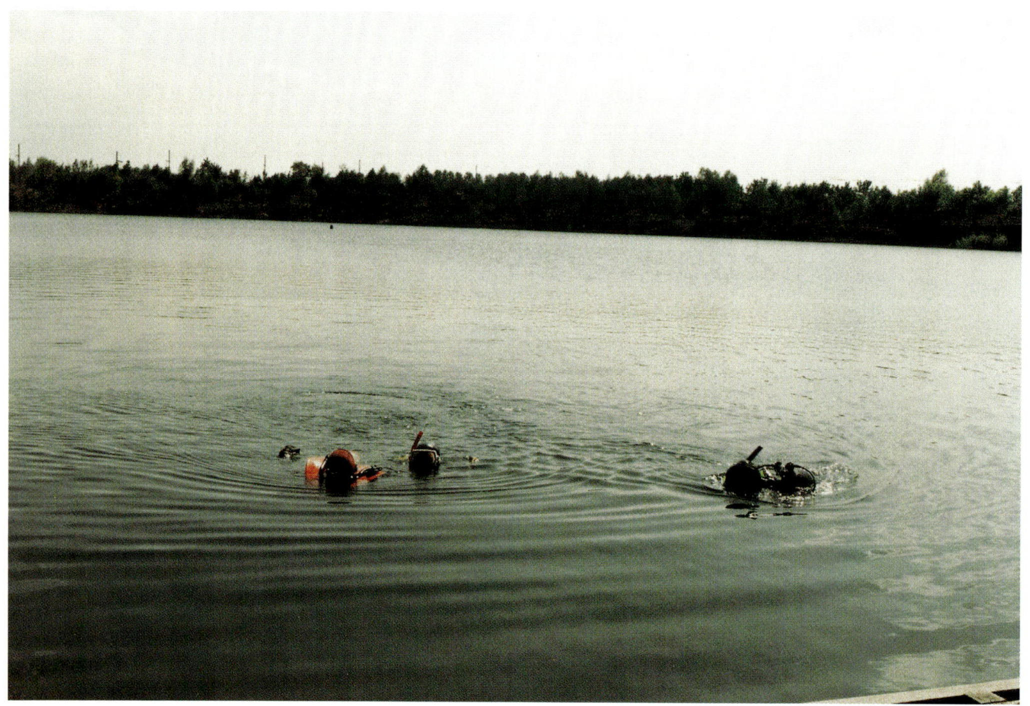

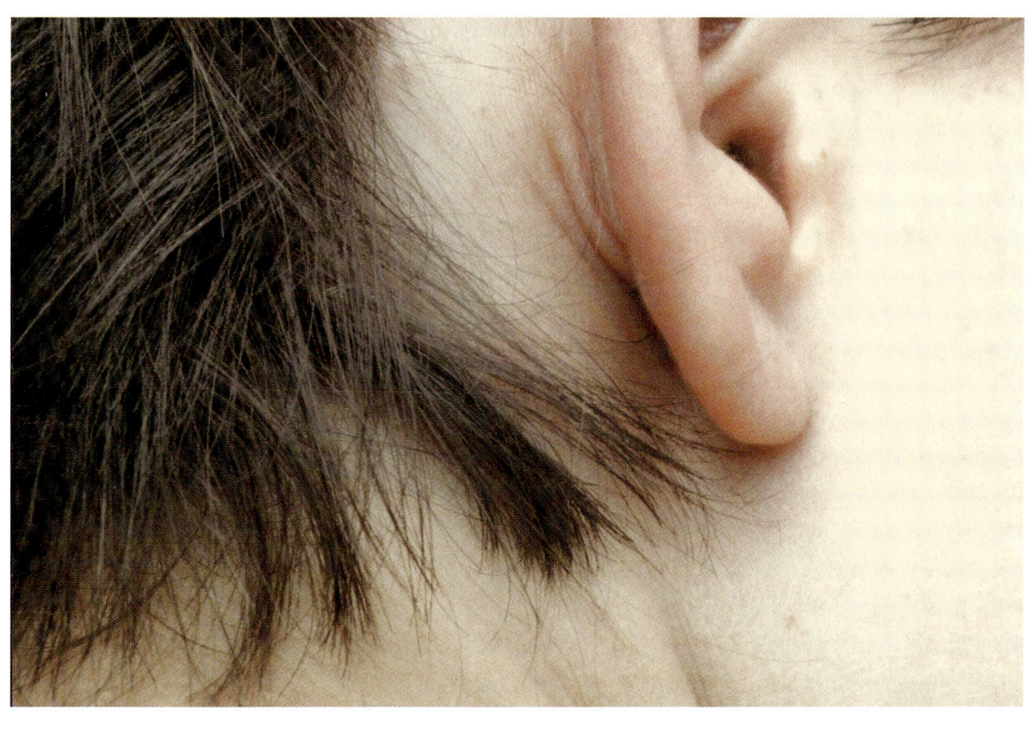

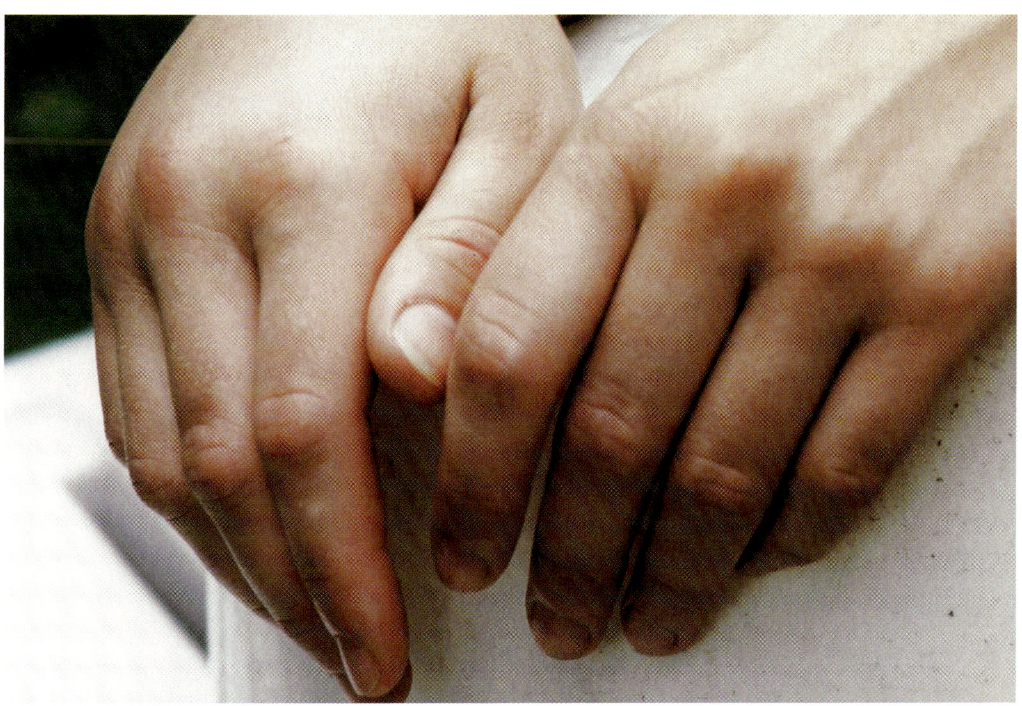

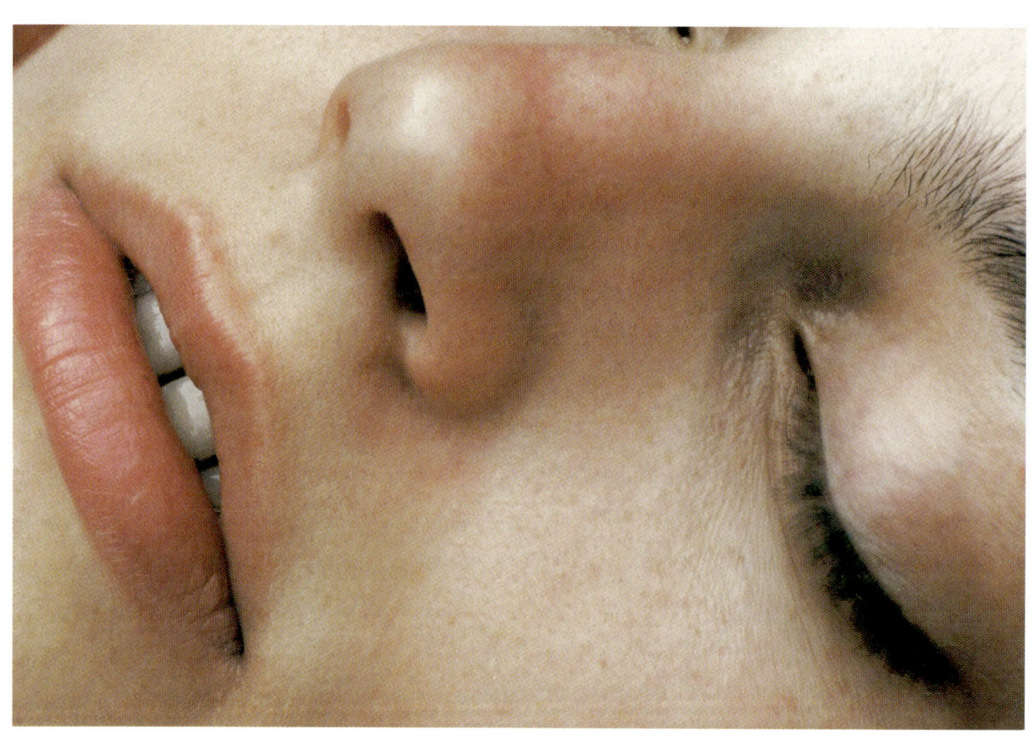

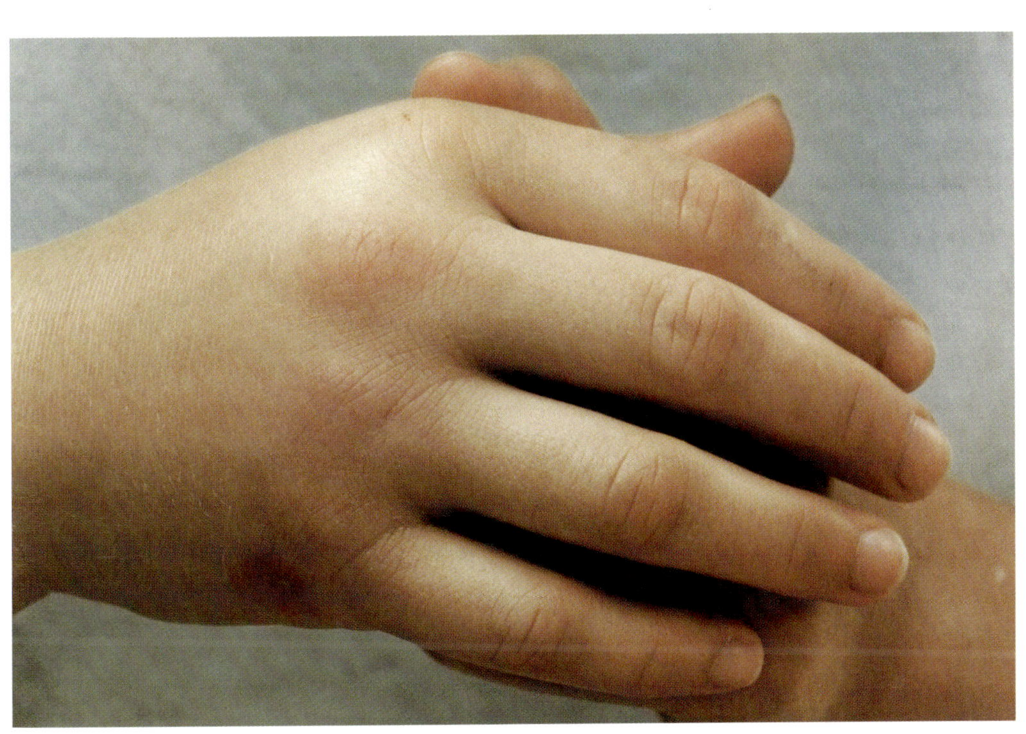

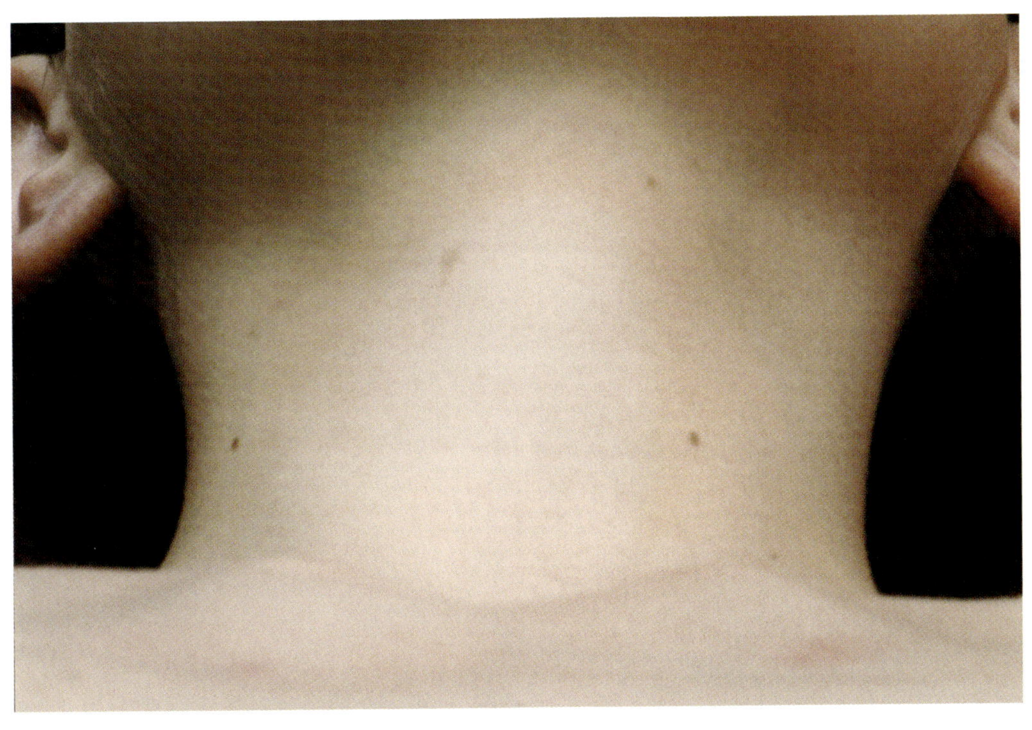

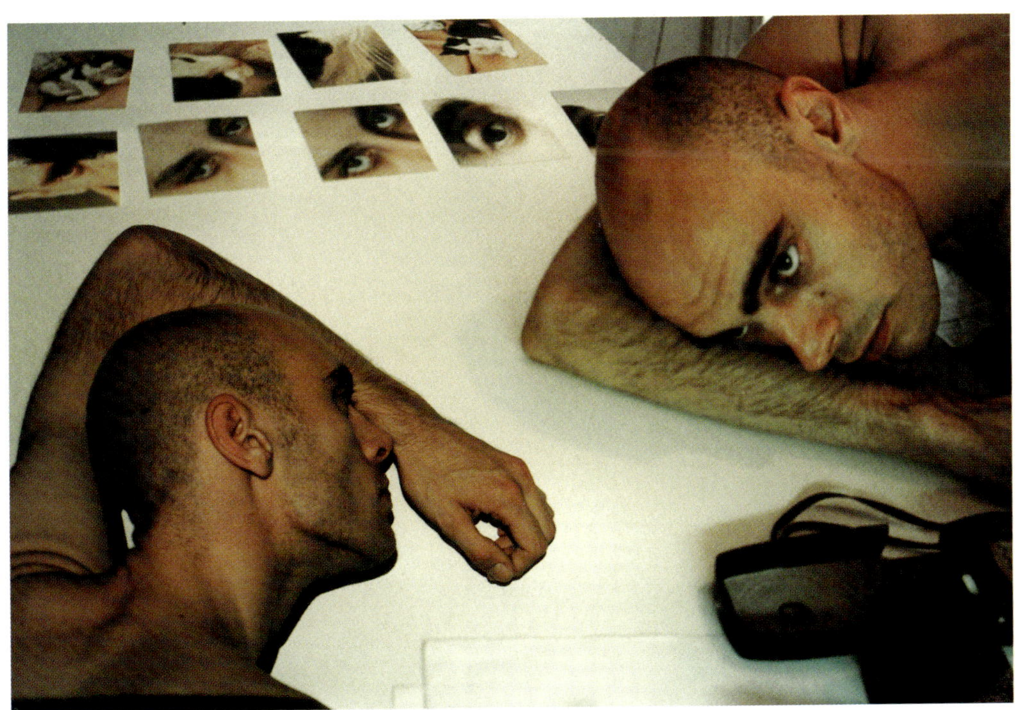

MARINA BONTRIDDER
PEUGEOT 404
AGATHA BLOEDVLOED
AUGUSTA FUTURA
FUTURA VISAVIS
ANN AALGOED
IRMA ISRAA
CAMELIA DEDOODT
ARISVRELIS
ADIEU

HEBBEN
OVERSCHOT
VAN
GELIJK !

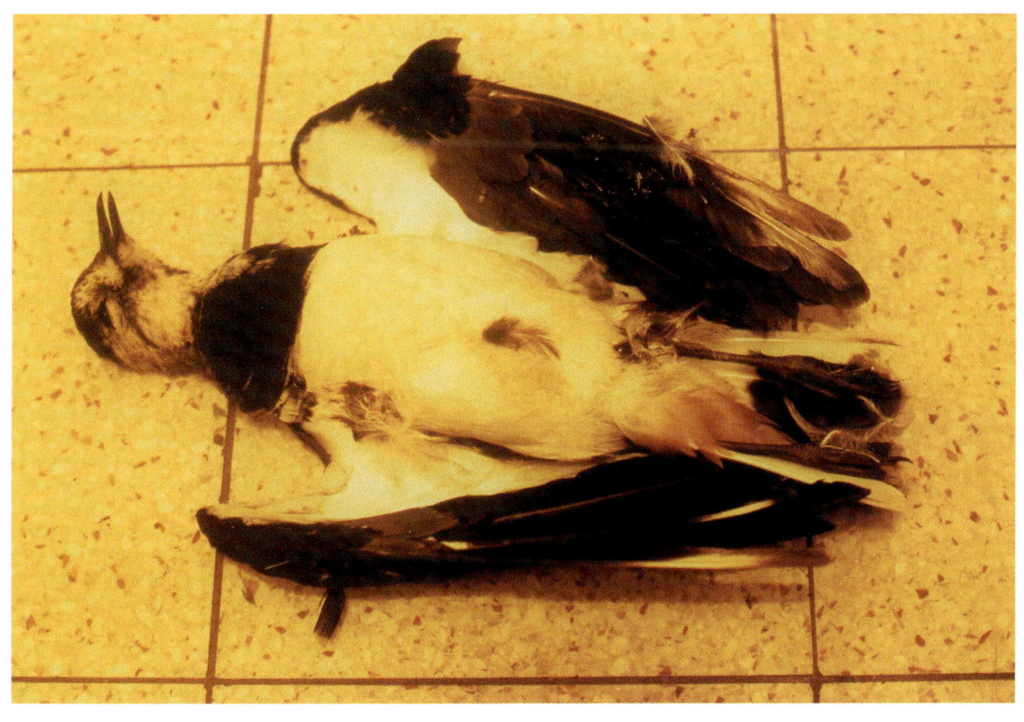

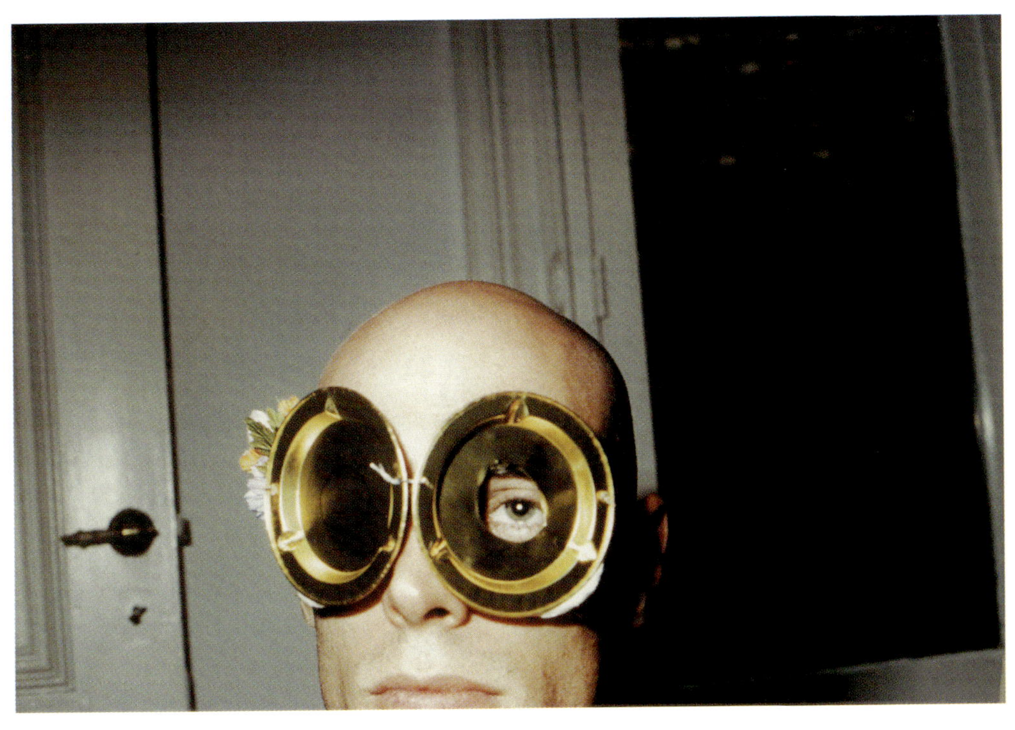

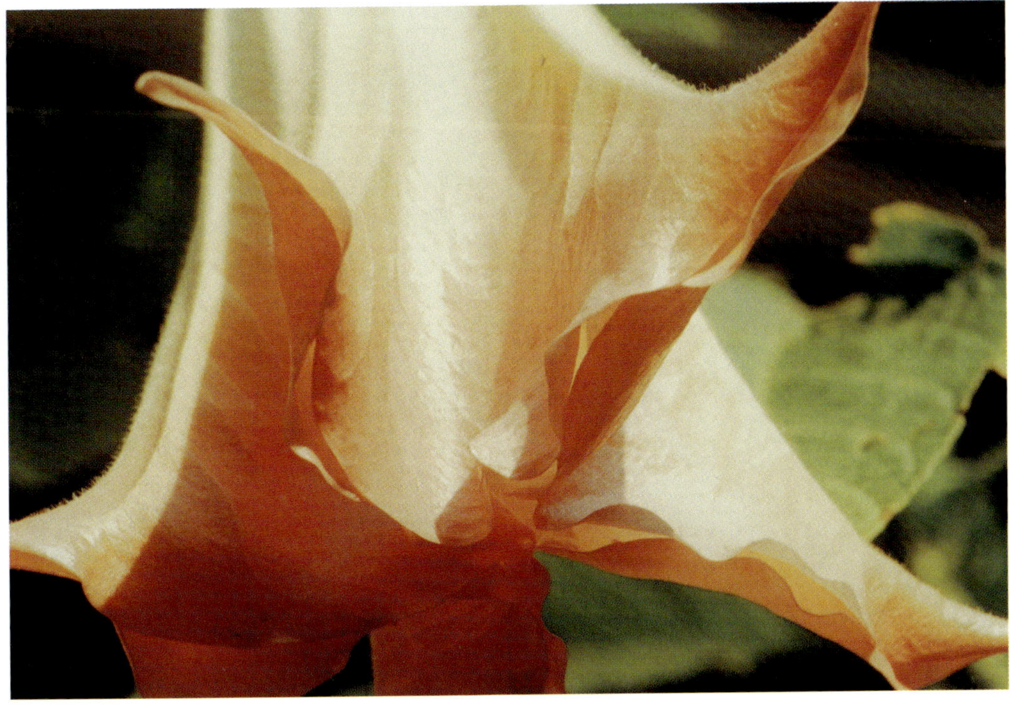

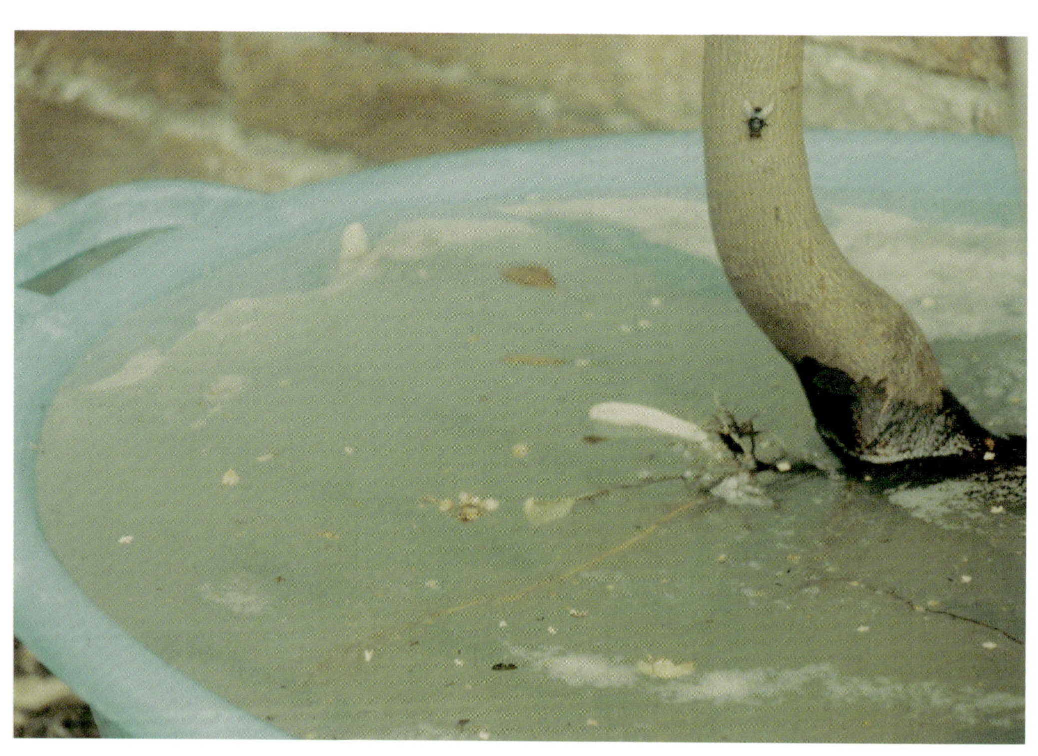

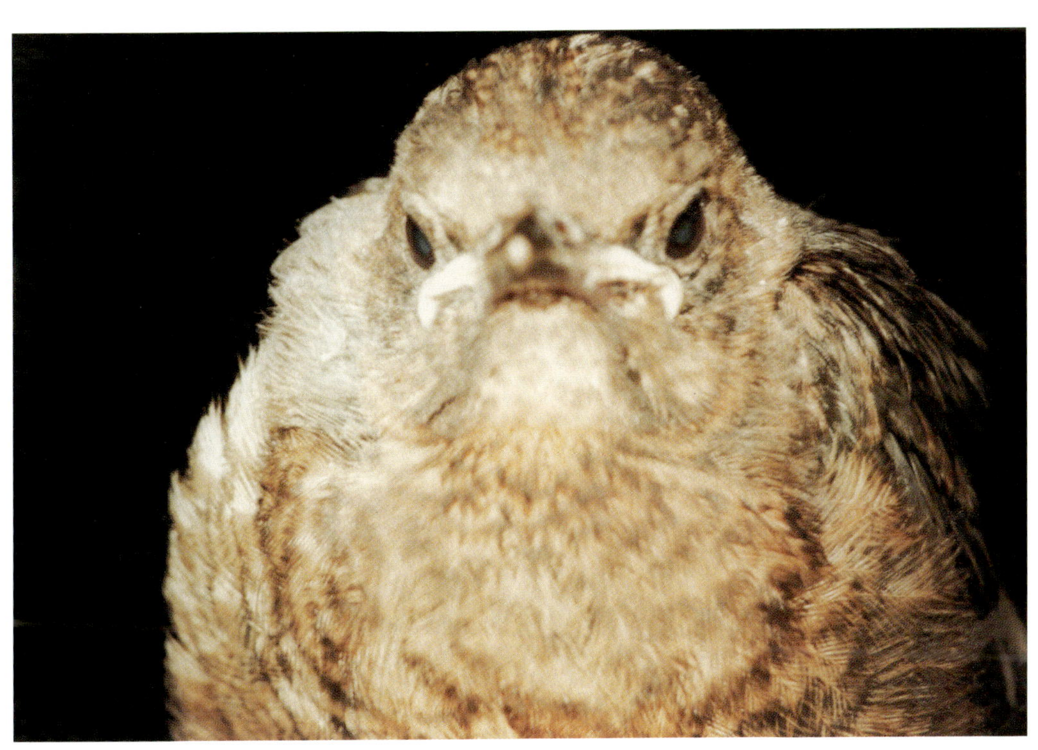

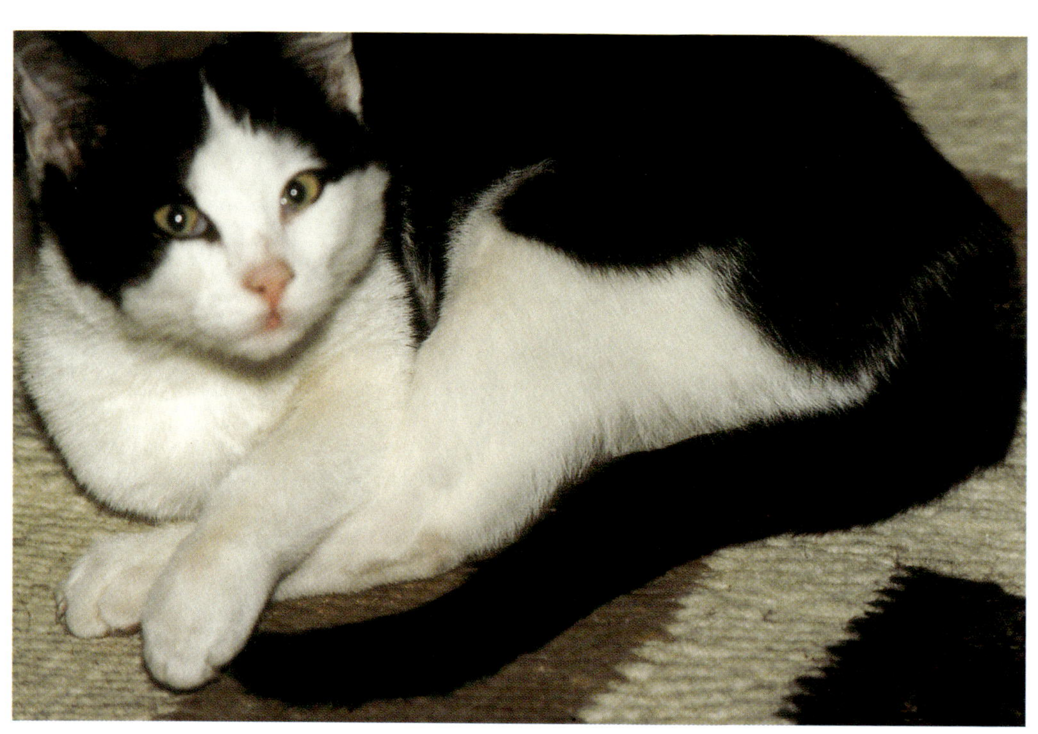

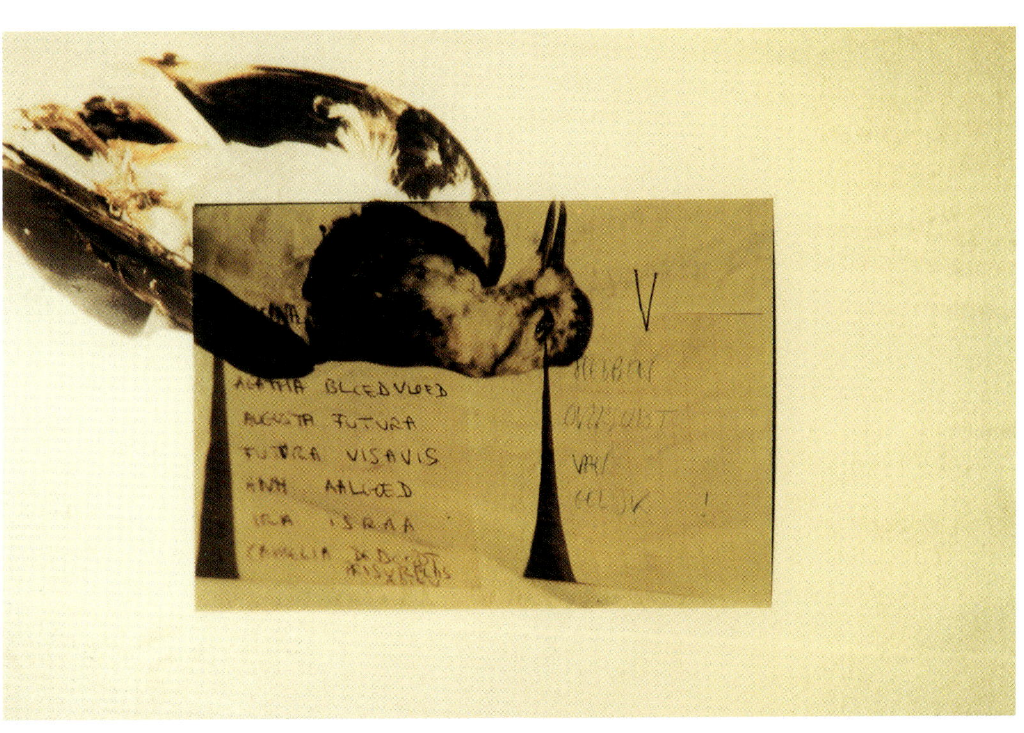

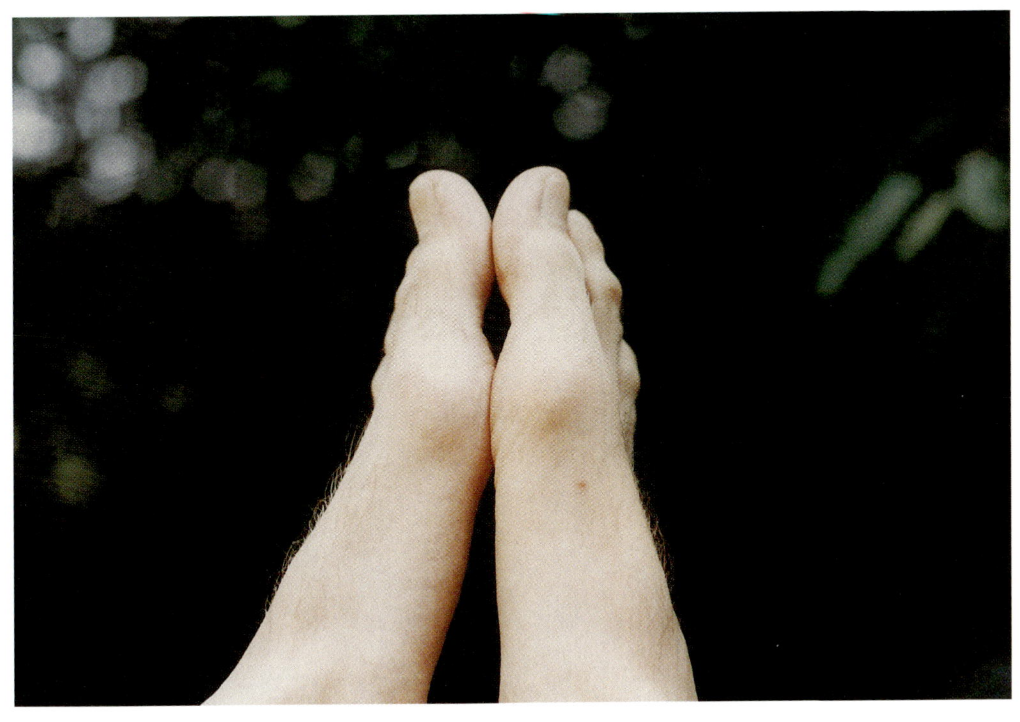

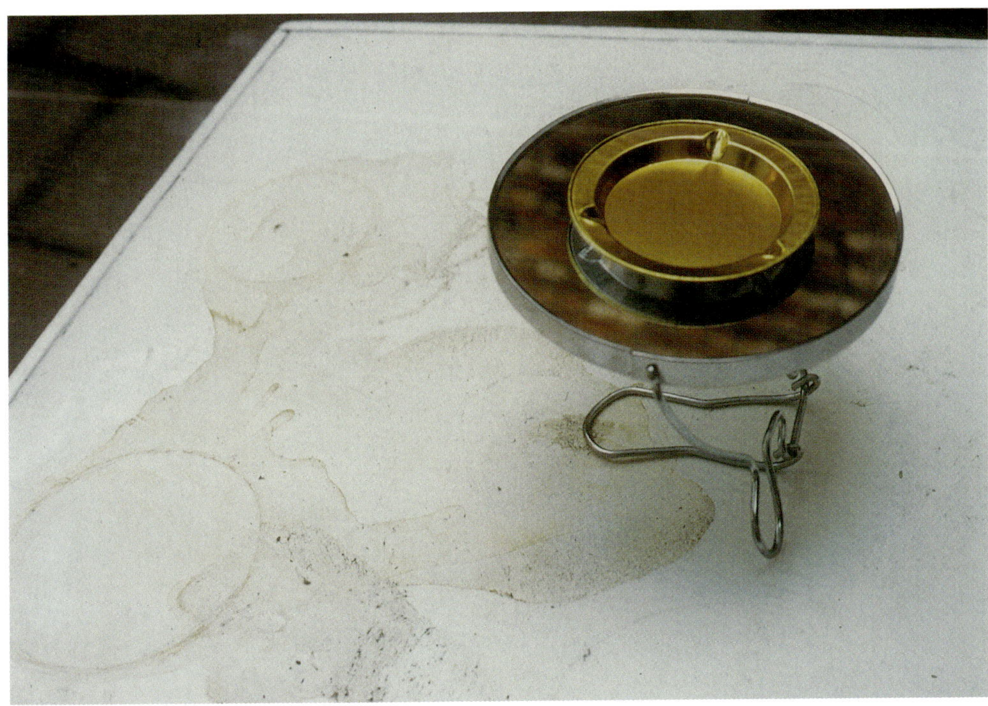

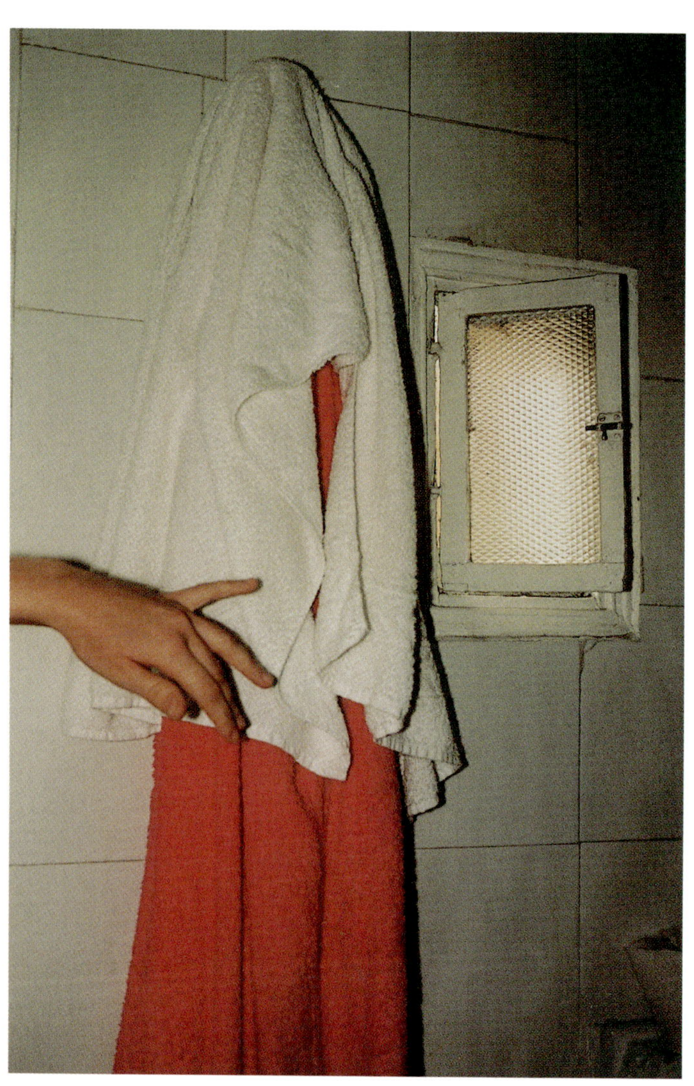

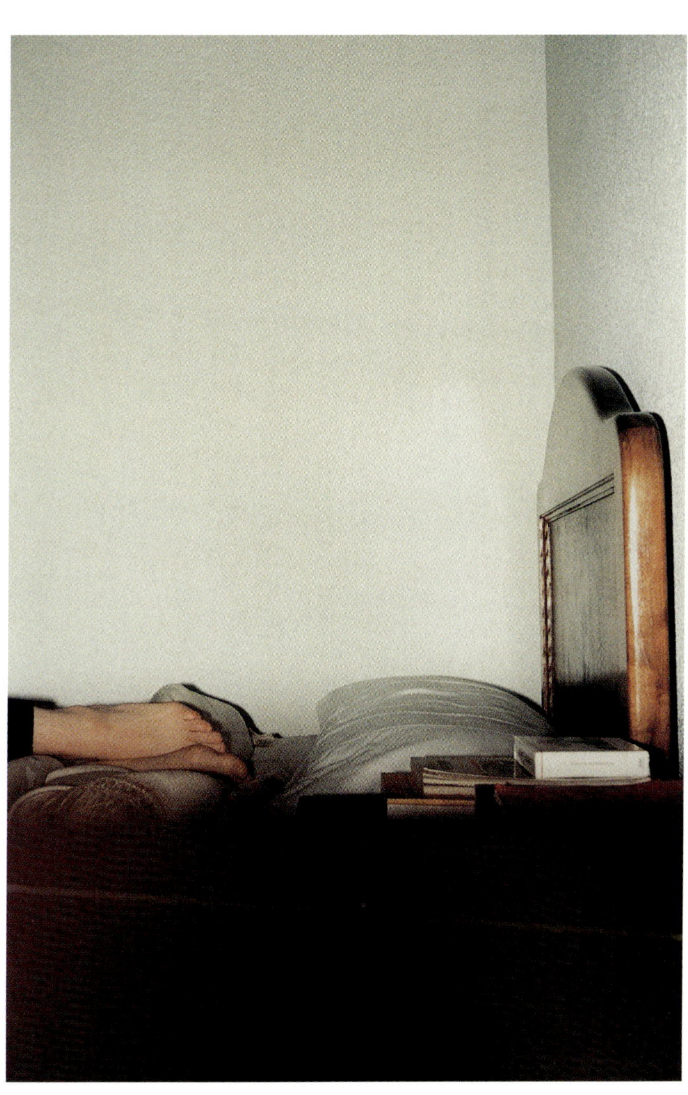

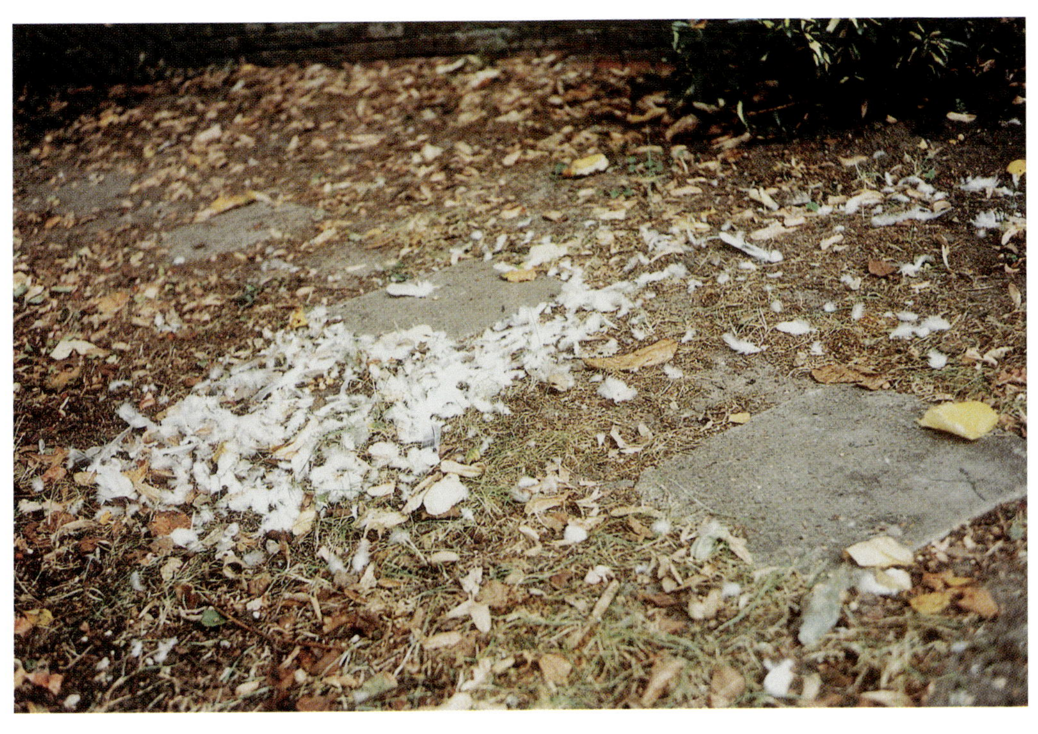

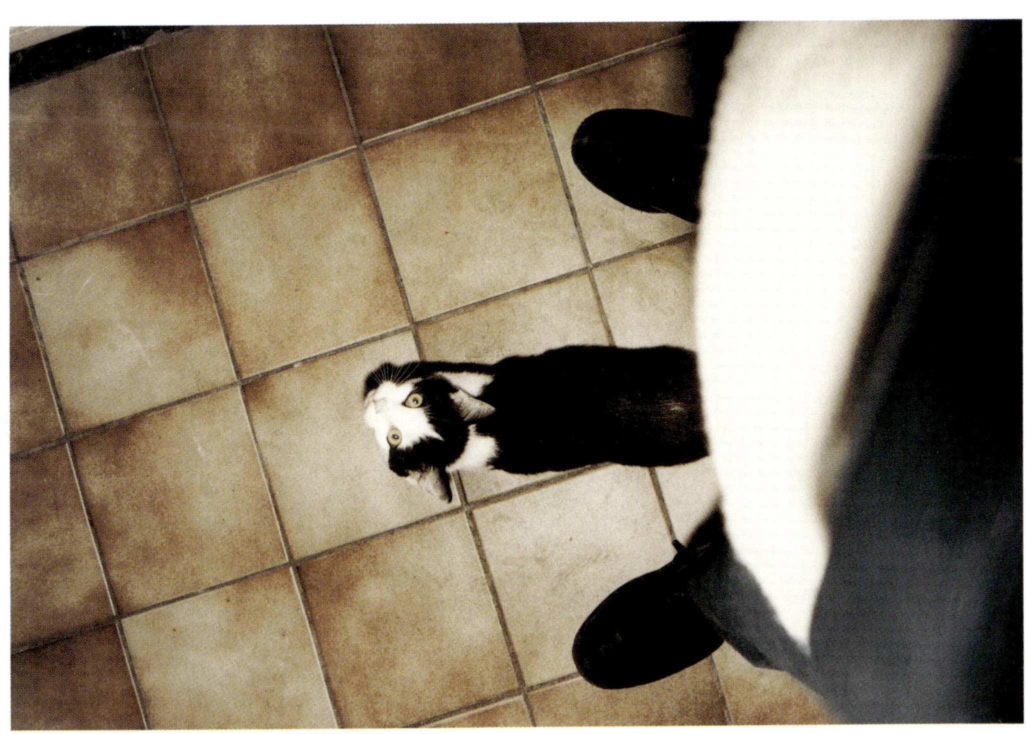

I am very pleased to present this publication, which comprises an important part of Jan de Vries' work, to the public.

Jan de Vries lived and worked in Belgium. In 1996 he died, aged thirty, in St.Martens-Latem.
As an artist De Vries was best known for his sculptures and installations; his photographic work only developed at a later stage and was never exhibited by himself.
The book was started in 1995 and discontinued shortly before he died. The original is an A4 sketch book, composed by De Vries, who selected for it some of his own photographs in order to create an interrelating whole. This edition comprises the complete original photo book, unchanged.

It contains pictures of De Vries' everyday life, taken in the places he was staying or passing through.

I first met Jan de Vries three and a half years before his death. He asked me to assist him in preparing and mounting an exhibition. Not only did this meeting eventually lead to a close friendship, but also to our continuous supplementation to each other's work and vision. The publication of this book fits within this specific relationship; it also affords the opportunity to draw attention to his artistic heritage.

The original photo book did hot have an explicit title - 'Co-Relief' being one I have chosen myself. Co-relief means: the part among the other parts of the same relief.

TIMOTHY STAPPAERTS

KIKKABAU...KIKKABAU...*

i.

I have never met Jan de Vries, I have never seen one of his exhibitions:
I have seen only a few of his works, and this book. They have told me his
story. I believe I also know some of its intimate details. I don't want to go
into his drama, or whatever you want to call what it was that led him to an
early death. [*No quiero ver la sangre (...) sobre la arena.*]

But I have seen his book.

It brings to mind the title of a novel by Hugo Claus, *Het Verdriet van Belgie,*
and not only the title, but also its narrative content, and even, and especially,
its structure, circular and irreversible at the same time. With Jan de Vries's
book too, once we reach the end, we may want to start over again and make
those changes we consider necessary with the benefit of hindsight: we may
feel the urgency to tell him about them, even though all communication
with him in person has been cut off for ever, as a result of his irrevocable
decision. It is, however, equally certain that no adjustment is possible.
[*Rewind.*] What is done is done, and if this is the result, a result that makes
sense only in its conclusion, only after often fallacious first impressions,
this is it. ["*Demand me nothing: what you know, you know:/ from this time
forth I never will speak word.*"]

ii.

An age-old tradition, from van Eyck to Huysmans, seems to be rooted in
Belgian culture – or perhaps it would be better to say Flemish, if it weren't for
the continual overflow and contamination of surrounding areas, and thus
Belgian – according to which reality derives from the sum of its parts; or,
from another point of view, representation of reality is derived from partial
and specific representations of its parts. To a unitary vision, that of the Italian
Renaissance, for example, according to which the whole gives meaning to the
parts of which it is made up, corresponds a complementary vision according
to which the integrated addition of the parts gives meaning to the whole.

---

* For the Greeks the cry of the night-owl, as transcribed by Giovanni Pascoli in one of his *Poemi Conviviali,*
entitled *La civetta,* which describes, after Plato's *Critone,* the death of Socrates: it is a good omen.

That this vision, then, may derive from a model of society, that of the artisans and merchants of the city emerging as the new centre of social life at the waning of the feudal world, and thus from the rise of the bourgeoisie as active citizens and principal instruments of the city's growth – while in Italy the monocentric model remained, whether pragmatically theocratic or nostalgically imperial, the ideal background to the analagous phenomenon of the rebirth of the artisan and mercantile cities –, remains a plausible hypothesis, even though here not put forward as analytically and scientifically deduced and demonstrated.

In the same way I propose the hypothesis that from this long-lived cultural attitude derives another phenomenology that emerges in the sphere of Belgian art in the century just past and that until now has shown no signs of being dismissed.

From James Ensor through Magritte and Marcel Broodthaers to Jan Vercruysse and Thierry De Cordier, but likewise detectable in a large number of other contemporary artists, from Guillaume Bijl to Luc Tuymans, a constant is evident, which at first glance would seem to take on the character of an obsession with objects, with objects/image, with images/object. I mean that numerous and various objects are transformed in the work of these artists into images without divesting them of their own objectness, that is, retaining certain of their essential characteristics, in different ways each time according to the specificity of the work of each artist. I would identify three of these essential characteristics, well aware there may be others here less appropriate to the purpose of the argument:
materiality: a transient materiality that wears out over time and to which, as such it is subject – every material thing is subject to time – but also subject to alterations and *trompe l'oeil*: its appearance may not be its substance, and its substance may be altered to the point that it may appear to be different from what it is effectively;
symbolic nature: every object, object/image, image/object, has become the bearer of meanings, more or less explicit, sometimes more uncanny than mysterious, either because of their form or their use;
non-oneness: which is manifested in their presence in many examples in the contexts of life and, publicly and privately, in everyday iconography.
I'm thinking of Ensor's flowers and shells, of Magritte's *petit bourgeois* bric-à-brac, of Broodthaers's eggshells and mussel shells, of the wide repertoire of symbolic objects that appear in the photographic works of Vercruysse, of the soiled and time-worn objects that characterise De Cordier's anti-modern iconography. It is more evident than it appears if you consider as polar

opposite the work of Bijl, whose compositions are made up only of objects, and that of Tuymans, whose painting dilutes the presence of objects by reducing them to their outlines or one of their surfaces, but doesn't renounce them completely.

If, then, an obsession with objects reflects a mindset based on a secular tradition typical of the Belgian cultural area, according to the hypothesis formulated above, its 'meaning' seems to me to be that of a simultaneous recognition and rejection. Recognition and rejection of the same thing: the vulgarity of existence (*Vorhandenheit*). A recognition and rejection that direct the act of the artist and the practice of art towards a sort of holding of existence to ransom: art is the positive overcoming of the negativity of existing. If in Ensor and also in Magritte we are dealing with a true process of sublimation, on the basis of Freudian analysis, and in Broodthaers of heroic acts undertaken by the individual/artist in his own titanic aspiration to totality – after Piero Manzoni and Joseph Beuys –, for Vercruysse and De Cordier it is a positive and melancholic affirmation of the sovereign singularity of the individual *tout court* in the moment in which he practises the discipline of art, whereas for Bijl and Tuymans it becomes a sceptical critique of the world and its representations.

The background remains the same for the book of photographs compiled by Jan de Vries one year before his death, and the book doesn't so much anticipate it as precede it and cannot be separated from it. I mean that the book does not negate the vulgarity of existing (*Vorhandenheit*), but the vulgarity of existing does not become the prime element with respect to the act that generated it, art, if you will; rather the act of Jan de Vries becomes a means of passing through the vulgarity of existing, and not of overcoming it in the ways I indicated above for the various artists.

[Rirkrit, in the cloistered silence of a night this autumn at the Castello, juxtaposed the term "flowing" with the term "attitude" evoked by Tobias; and I thought of the river that flows and which the boat follows towards the "heart of darkness". And I wasn't thinking any more of Kurtz: Kurtz had started to fade away like a distant idol.]

[When we entered the little tea house, Rirkrit stretched out on a tatami in front of the empty tokonoma and stayed there silent. When he got up and as we were leaving he said the house was beautiful.
The next day a Japanese artist came and placed a scroll in the tokonoma, made by himself, in order to begin to complete what was still missing. And with this addition the house shone.

*But I remember Rirkrit lying in front of the empty tokonoma and his words
afterwards. Not what is* missing, *because things may be what they have to be,
but what is in the instant they are visited.]*

This passing through neither saves nor redeems, but gives the sense of being
(*Dasein*) irreducible to pure and simple existence (*Vorhandenheit*). The light
implicit in the idea of *Dasein* corresponds to the panic and paradoxical
lucidity of Magritte, to Broodthaers's intellectual lucidity, to Vercruysse's
aesthetic lucidity, but it is not the same thing. In fact the active/passive
relationship – activity pleasure, passivity pain – from which the
negative/depressive drive derived, has been inverted, and was in any case
progressively enfeebled in the sequence of Magritte-Broodthaers-Vercruysse,
having assumed from time to time the romantic-decadent figures of the
scepsis, of titanism and of melancholy, respectively. Lucidity remains a
quality of looking, whereas light emanates from being, from *Dasein.*

In Jan de Vries there is no lucidity. His gaze is terse, but not lucid: the terse
look of someone who has put himself at a distance and receives everything
as a last gift. If there is no trace of understanding of the self, it is because
the Self has detached itself into a zone of transit; but there is, instead, a
profound and generous openness to being (*Erschlossenheit*), without the
expectation of anything in return. Indeed there is more pro-vocation than
pro-ject, and, even more than is required, there is recognition. The
technique and construction of the image are in the service of a revelation,
which is not "the flash of what saves", but the stillness of what is. There is
an attempt to put oneself to listening to what has been disconnected and
torn in the tension absolutely necessary in a form – it is of no importance at
this stage to distinguish between the form of production, of any production,
or that specific to art. This type of listening belongs to one who has
uprooted himself from every habitat [*Herentals*], including the habitat in
self-defence of the Self. In free fall towards the annihilation of the Self, the
book is a witness to the strata that are passed through in falling.

They are firstly in loose order, but not without any order, images from a cultural and personal repertoire that gives an account of an origin, of a condi-
tion lived, but which also anticipates a destiny pre-ordained down to the last
moves. And here everything has a density that admits neither space nor air.

Then a structure begins to take shape, a structure of voids, like a method
awaiting application. And already at this stage, the privileged position of the
observer is in the process of elimination: denial of perspective, evocation of
anamorphosis [*Holbein's* The Ambassadors], denunciation of gimmicks and

of deception. And all is achieved as if by a new method, a new perspective, a new possibility.

And so it is that, like an unexpected gift, things appear, reflexes, the inside and outside, beauty and the traces of its lonely poet, nature and its signs, physics and its ritual meanings, and each element is a part of a whole, and everything is everything: the animate and inanimate, the great and the small, the natural and the artificial, the unconsciousness and the production, a flight of birds and a hotel room, the whiskers of the cat and the wing of a fly, the one who feels and suffers and the one who moulds and gives shape, the one who is looked at and the look, black light and blind light, life death nothing the limit, the Self the non-Self the matter.

[*"Werd'ich zum Augenblicke sagen:/Verweile doch! Du bist so schön!/Dann..."*]

Yes, but one is falling [*"Sie stürzt, sie zerfällt!"*]. In free fall. So all this is memory? All this has been? So where was the substance of the presence of all this? Now the images confront each other demanding reason. [*La petite madeleine. Le temps perdu.*] I am falling. In the water that flows over the waterfall is my shadow. By now I am separate from *Everything* and *I* see *Myself* reflected in the window pane, and outside it's raining, raining. [*"...comme il pleut sur la ville."*]

Now there are only traces, which remain, beyond the time in which their apparition on the surface of the world is determined. Absent. But the games, the reflexes are multiple. Likewise in multiple directions falls the gaze. The third eye. The image of an image: the body and the sky, from low and from high, from the outside in, [*correspondances*] still what is repeated and what remains, what remains, who remains and who appears, spoils of after and figures from before, from before time that already doesn't belong. The figures, outside, from inside out, are confused, but what is lucidly clear is the absence, inside, from outside in. All of the Self begins to dissolve: *maquillage* of the image, body parts, and images, images of images, names of those who have never been and icon of what in the end could also be (a bird, or an angel, fallen), water (the dirty water after the baby has been thrown away) and the nocturnal bird (chick or bird of prey?). I see you looking at me without memory and a text so vague that it is also a testament. Here is what I see: only the parts in motion or at rest. The fall is over, I've seen it, you've seen it, *petit chat*, die away.

Kikkabau...kikkabau...

PIER LUIGI TAZZI
Brussels and Capalle, summer-autumn 2000

The publishers wish to thank Eric and Flora Stappaerts, and
Inge Henneman, Museum for Photography, Antwerp.

Edited by Timothy Stappaerts
Book design by Luc Derycke
Texts: Timothy Stappaerts, Pier-Luigi Tazzi
Translations: James Douglas, Ferdinand du Bois

All photographs in this book were taken by Jan de Vries, except for the 3 images
marked by asterisks, taken by Timothy Stappaerts.

A MERZ publication

MERZ is a joint imprint of Luc Derycke & Co., Marrot NV. and Tijdsbeeld NV.,
and is open to other publishers.

Published by
Timothy Stappaerts
Acacialaan 13
B-2020 Antwerpen, Belgium.
T +32 478 72 67 95
and
MERZ/Luc Derycke & Co.
Lange Steenstraat 10
B 9000 Gent
T + 32 9 329 31 22/F +32 9 329 31 23

ISBN: 90-6917-005-1

Wettelijk depot nr. D/2000/7852/6

Distributed in Europe by Exhibitions International
Kol. Bégaultlaan, 17
B 3012 Leuven, Belgium
T +32 16 29 69 00/F +32 16 29 61 29

Distributed, in the US, by D.A.P.
155 Sixth Avenue
New York, NY 10013-1507
T 212-627-1999/F 212-627-9484

Printed and bound in Belgium

Published with the support of the Ministery of the Flemish Community,
Administration for Culture.